Columbia University

Contributions to Education

Teachers College Series

No. 810

AMS PRESS

NEW YORK

A Study of Mothers' Practices and Children's Activities in a Co-operative Nursery School

BY CLARA TUCKER, Ph.D.

TEACHERS COLLEGE, COLUMBIA UNIVERSITY
CONTRIBUTIONS TO EDUCATION, NO. 810

Bureau of Publications
Teachers College · Columbia University
New York · 1940

Library of Congress Cataloging in Publication Data

Tucker, Clara, 1897-
    A study of mothers' practices and children's acti-
vities in a co-operative nursery school.

    Reprint of the 1940 ed., issued in series: Teachers
College, Columbia University. Contributions to educa-
tion, no. 810.
    Originally presented as the author's thesis,
Columbia.
    Bibliography: p.
    1. Parent and child. 2. Nursery schools.
3. Mothers. 4. Child study. I. Title. II. Series:
Columbia University, Teachers College. Contributions
to education, no. 810.
HQ769.T8 1972   372.21'6   79-177696

ISBN 0-404-55810-0

HQ
769
.T8
1972

EDUCATION
LIBRARY

Reprinted by Special Arrangement with Teachers
College Press, New York, New York

From the edition of 1940, New York
First AMS edition published in 1972
Manufactured in the United States

AMS PRESS, INC.
NEW YORK, N. Y.   10003

ACKNOWLEDGMENTS

THE writer wishes to acknowledge her indebtedness to Dr. Arthur T. Jersild, who guided the development of this study, and to express her appreciation for his suggestions and criticisms.

She is grateful to Dr. Lois Hayden Meek and to Dr. Robert S. Lynd for their interest in the study and for their helpful suggestions.

To the members of the Co-operative Nursery School in which the experiment was carried out, the writer wishes to express her gratitude for the co-operation which made the study possible.

C. T.

CONTENTS

Contents

Chapter I

INTRODUCTION

OLD AND NEW EMPHASES IN PARENT EDUCATION

FOR the past two decades much emphasis has been placed by educators upon the preparation of the individual for parenthood, and upon the education of the parent for the experiences which are a part of family life. In reviewing the history of parent education during this period, the writer sought answers to the following questions: (1) What problems in parent education have been included in the curriculum for parental training? (2) What methods have been used? (3) How effective have the programs been? (4) What constructive changes have been evidenced in the more recent educational theories which are applicable to the effective training of parents?

An examination of the problems included in parent education during this period revealed that the reasons why they have been considered by the experts as pertinent to parent education are not clear. Theoretically, the problems selected as bases for pre-parental and parental training are those of the parent either in preparation for family life or for establishing a more satisfactory family life. The history of the development of parent education reveals a shifting of emphasis in the nature of the problems involved as well as an interest in the development of special activities which have been and are making important contributions to a more adequate home life. For example, in the early history of parent education, problems were mainly those of physical care and improvement of physical conditions of family members; the management of problems of the family became the next center of interest. The latest development has been emphasis upon the emotional problems of the family group—the problems of relationships. Another source of confusion, which apparently the earlier leaders of parent education failed to recognize, was the basis for

1

considering problems pertinent to pre-parental training or for establishing a more satisfactory family life.

In the endeavors to understand and change the child's behavior, the child himself has often been the starting point. From an objective point of view, this approach shows a lack of insight into the real problem. If the problem is approached objectively, the first question should be, What is the basis for calling the child's behavior a problem? Second, Why is the child's behavior unsatisfactory in the relationship which he is attempting to establish? The answer to the first question may be found in the personal and social attitudes of the individual—the adult—who has pointed out that the child's behavior is a problem. The second question also concerns attitudes. The answer is determined by the standards of acceptability of children's behavior set up by the social order. In other words, it is impossible to separate the consideration of a child's behavior from the standards of those who judge him, for those standards are the bases of adult attitudes toward him.

Merely pointing out to the parent an objectionable attitude is not enough; he needs assistance in establishing practices and techniques which will function constructively in solving problems and forming satisfactory relationships between himself and his child. It is too much to expect that the untrained (and often the trained) parent can express his attitude toward the child in consistently constructive and comprehensible language. However, the understanding of children and their problems, and of relationships as they should exist in the family, is essential for the parent if improvement in family life is to result. Parents of "problem children" need to be skillfully and sympathetically guided in acquiring the techniques with which to meet the problems of family life.

The importance of the influence exerted by the parents and family on the formation of the child's attitudes and behavior is closely paralleled by that of the teacher and the school. However, because of differences in experimental backgrounds between parents and teachers, their reactions to the problems of the child's adjustment differ unless a point of view common to both has been established and a similar program of education for the guidance of the child has been undertaken.

It is important, therefore, that the individual most responsible for the child's guidance should investigate first the obstacles that retard the development of the child's personality. Then results of this investigation should be interpreted to the family, the school, and the community agencies actively engaged in child guidance, and effective techniques should be established as a basis for this guidance. Guidance based upon a complete picture of the child's behavior has already been undertaken by groups interested in parent education, but the work has been handicapped by a lack of agreement and by an inadequate understanding on the part of those involved, of both the child's problems and those of the family.

REVIEW OF LITERATURE

The recognition that attitudes and practices are important in the early development of the individual has led various investigators to study intensively these two basic factors. Studies have been made of the various situations in which the adult and the child come in contact at home and at school, and these situations have been evaluated from different points of view and by different persons: the parent, the teacher, the mental hygienist, and the specialist. The discussion which follows deals only with a limited list of studies, most of which were published when this study was begun in 1931, and those studies, published later, selected because of the contribution made to the understanding of practices used by mothers in directing children of pre-school age.

In studies made by Laws [7]* and by Tilson [12], attitudes and practices of parents are accepted as functionally related to the responses of the child.

The results of Laws' study revealed that certain parental prejudices apparently influence the ratings of children's responses to the practices of parents. The group of parents studied tended

---

* The numbers in brackets throughout the study refer to corresponding numbers in the Bibliography, pages 165-166.

to rate the children's responses to practices somewhat lower than did the observers. However, as Laws pointed out, the relation between practice and response was rated higher by parents in cases where "the response of the child is a source of irritation to the parent, when the response is a higher standard demanded by the parent than by the observer, or when the response of the child is likely to make a better showing before persons outside the family" (p. 22). The results also show the importance of the relationship existing between the attitudes and practices of the parent and the responses of the child. The findings of this study suggest that it is difficult to obtain accurate data from parents concerning the relationship between their practices and the behavior of their children.

Tilson, in her study, *The Problems of the Pre-school Child* [12], investigated, among other problems, the types of undesirable parental attitudes and practices and the frequency of their occurrence. The seven problems which most frequently occur in children were studied in relation to nine of the parental attitudes and practices which were reported as most undesirable. The results show that a positive relationship exists between the problems of children of pre-school age and the attitudes and practices of their parents.[1]

Dennis [3] made a study of thirty-six families in three types of environment: namely, twenty families in a city of 20,000 persons, ten in a village of 150 inhabitants, and six in a rural community. Her conclusion is that the success with which parents are able to make adjustments and solve the problems of relationships between themselves and their children appears to be related to the following parental attitudes: (1) the degree to which parents respect their children as individuals; (2) the extent to which they understand their children's need for companionship, not only with themselves but with other children (in order to live a normal play life and to find opportunities for the development of independ-

[1] It is interesting to note that the most undesirable parental practice, as shown by the data obtained from seven guidance clinics and interpreted by Tilson, is "disagreement on discipline," and that a domineering attitude toward the child produces the least serious result.

ence); and (3) the degree to which they take into account the physical and emotional limitations of the child.

The studies of Tilson and of Dennis deal with attitudes which make for maladjustments between parents and children, but their report does not indicate the processes whereby particular parent practices and techniques create undesirable attitudes toward the child.

Research workers in fields other than the pre-school have investigated the parent-child relationship as a determinant in the emotional level of adjustment of the individual. In Maller's character sketches [8] and in Chassell's *Experience Variable* [2], questions are included on parent-child relationship. The deductions drawn from the results establish the parent-child relationship as a determinant in the emotional adjustment of the individual.

Answers to a questionnaire study made by Watson [13] on the subject of happiness also show that the relationship which exists between the individual and his parents in early life is one of the determining factors in that individual's happiness in adult life.

In a recent study by Humphrey [4], a relationship was shown to exist between the child and his early life in the home and the play behavior of a group of twenty-one children ranging in age from two years eleven months to four years one month.

Analyses of correlations between parental protection versus rejection and child behavior patterns suggest that either extreme of protection or rejection tends to foster simple planless activity and lack of perseverance. The results of the present study also indicate that home environments encouraging self-expression tend to correlate with such patterns of child behavior as ease of stimulation in play, increased perseverance, and greater constructive complex activity.

Two studies which illustrate how attitudes unquestionably affect the methods used in endeavoring to help the child to solve his problems of adjustment and to build wholesome relationships between children and adults are those of Wickman and Stogdill.

In an investigation of the relationships between the attitudes of a representative group of teachers and those of a group of mental hygienists toward children's behavior problems, Wickman [14] found that the differences, expressed in ratings obtained from a group of teachers and a group of mental hygienists, could be interpreted as differences in opinion as to the "seriousness" of the particular behavior in its effect upon the child's adjustment. Mental hygienists considered the unsocial forms of behavior more serious and placed less stress upon examples of anti-social behavior, which, as a rule, the teachers considered significant. The teachers considered problems relating to dishonesty, disobedience, disorderliness, sex, and failure to learn as the most serious, while the mental hygienists rated withdrawing and recessive characteristics of a child as representing the most serious obstacles to its adjustment.

Stogdill [11] made a study of the attitudes of parents and hygienists in order to find how much importance each attached to children's various behavior problems. The results show that the mental hygienists considered fear, depression, cruelty, and whining as indicative of more serious disorders than did the parents; while the parents considered habits involving disobedience, lying, stealing, and masturbation as indicative of more serious disorders.

The studies made by Wickman and Stogdill suggest that conflicting opinions as to the seriousness of the child's problems imply disagreement concerning the methods of guidance and of treatment of behavior disorders by the two groups that are most influential in effecting a basis for stable emotional growth in the child. The results of these two studies imply the importance of consistency in training children in forming acceptable behavior patterns along with the importance attached to consistency in a program for treating behavior disorders of the child.

Dr. Ojeman [9], at the University of Iowa Child Welfare Research Station, has attempted to discover the needs of parent groups and has planned a curriculum to meet these needs. The three studies discussed in the following paragraphs are associated with Dr. Ojeman's investigation in this field.

In the first study, Ackerley [1] investigated the parents' needs, planned a curriculum that was designed to be scientifically adapted to these needs, and also attempted to evaluate the progress made by the parents during the period of observation. In this study generalizations were collected from various sources on the mental, emotional, social, and physical development of the child, the use of money, sex education, and vocational guidance. These generalizations were evaluated by judges who had knowledge of the practical problems involved, as well as of the technical background, on the basis of their importance to parents of children in the elementary school. The results show that the answers of 774 parents who had instruction in the problems included in the study revealed a lack of comprehension of the problem as judged by the experts. The results also show the inability of parents to use the generalizations understandingly, a deficiency that was not confined to any one field investigated.

Schaus [10] made a study of the relative advantages of the lecture method and the discussion method in the instruction of parents. To obtain the necessary data, she gave tests on information and practices to two groups of parents, after which one group was instructed by the lecture method and the other by the discussion method. At the end of the course both groups were again tested, and it was found that both had raised their scores on the information tests, but that the tests on changes in practices did not indicate important differences.

Jack [5] developed an instrument for scoring parental practices and children's behavior to be used in evaluating results of a course in parent education. She reports that the average change, as shown by the scores, was not great enough to indicate improvement; however, the mothers who originally had ranked lowest showed the most improvement.

The measure of the effectiveness of a parent education program is based upon changes found in the parents' knowledge and attitudes, as shown in their methods of meeting the problems of child guidance. The findings of Lashley, in his studies of personality and attitude scales [6], indicate that, in order to give satisfactory results, measures of the types just described must be supplemented by other measures of behavior. Until research has established the relationship between opinion and behavior upon a satisfactory basis, many of the findings of the investigators just discussed will remain inconclusive.

PROBLEMS IN PARENT EDUCATION REVEALED BY MODERN RESEARCH

If we judge parent education from the standpoint of the few facts known about the specificity of learning, it would seem that educators in this field have not dealt adequately with the obstacles that parents must overcome in adapting new learnings to their family situations. The ability to acquire knowledge and recognize facts represents one type of development; to apply knowledge so acquired to the changing of stubborn habits requires a different kind of development. When the attempts to educate parents are viewed from the standard set up by the parent educator, namely, that real learning be evidenced in the parents' behavior, it becomes apparent that other methods and devices are required in order to enable the parent to apply his knowledge to his problems, which include himself, his child, his family, and his community.

Research in the field of parent education also shows that the program for this specialized education has its limitations when measured by recognized educational standards.

Among developments in parent education that may be sought at this time are (1) a clearer, more comprehensive knowledge of each parent's problems, as viewed from every angle, in his or her relation to the family and its members; (2) concerted action by agencies interested in parent education in the formulation of a program for pre-parental and parental training; and (3) the application of some of the recent and progressive advances made in the educational field to the education of both parent and child that should bring about a more harmonious group relationship.

THE CO-OPERATIVE NURSERY SCHOOL

The co-operative nursery school is an experimental approach to the education of the parent through demonstration. The organization of the school is one in which the parent and the child are actively interested and one in which they work co-operatively toward the solution of their problems. A solution is sought for many problems which involve changes in behavior—evidence of learning on the part of the parent and of the child. Each is given guidance in the solution of his problems as an individual and as a member of the group. In the co-operative school there is an appreciable opportunity for close association between the home and the school in the problems to be solved by the child.

Education for family life through the experience gained in the co-operative nursery school applies methods advocated by the more progressive leaders in the educational field of today. Personal growth, which has been and still is the keynote of the philosophy of the progressive education movement, when consciously sought makes the education of the parent an interesting experience both for the parent and for the child.

In many of the nurseries and pre-schools organized most recently for the education of family members, much thought has been given to the consistency of the training program from the viewpoint of the parent as well as of the child. Two schools of this type were studied as a means of understanding the organization and methods used in a co-operative pre-school center.

The University of Chicago Nursery School.[2] When it was organized in 1916, the University of Chicago Nursery School had as its chief concern the problem of the family. A small group of women worked out a plan for co-operative care of children in the University of Chicago community. After the group had secured a home in a gymnasium, the University showed its interest in the school by supplying funds for equipment and providing heat, light, and janitorial service. In 1923 the Cooperative Nursery School purchased a three-story house, acquired through gifts and the financial assistance of the University. In 1929, with the help of gifts and funds from the University, an adjoining piece of property was bought with the understanding that the property was to be used jointly by the Nursery School and the University for educational purposes.

The Nursery School was designed to provide, for a limited

[2] *The University Cooperative Nursery School,* pp. 3-5. Staff members of the University of Chicago Cooperative Nursery School, University of Chicago, 1936-1937.

number of hours each week, an opportunity for mothers to learn more about the behavior of the individual child, to observe the methods used by those skilled in the guidance of children in their behavior problems, and to participate, under supervision, in the management of children. The school was designed to function, too, as an education experience for the pre-school child.

The Smith College Co-operative Nursery School.[3] Another co-operative nursery school in which parents and children are interested in family life problems is the school developed at Smith College under the supervision of the Institute for Co-ordination of Women's Interests. The purpose of the Institute is to help the educated woman to use those special powers which cost money, time, and effort to develop, and which she often tends to discard after marriage. The principles on which the Institute was founded and the methods which it uses grew out of the recognition that special skills and powers constitute valuable social material which needs to be conserved. The young educated woman, who is very often unhappy over the lack of opportunity to use her powers, should be given the opportunity to continue to use them.

A co-operative nursery school was decided upon as a practical demonstration which would furnish these mothers an opportunity to secure training in the solution of their own problems and also serve as a means of demonstrating the possibilities of such a project to any group of parents who were willing to accept the attendant responsibilities.

The Co-operative Nursery School was organized in May, 1926, and was opened in September, 1926. As was originally planned, there were to be fifteen children, under the care of a nursery school teacher, a nursery school mother who was engaged to prepare and serve the food, and a second nursery school mother, a trained nurse, who would spend one-half of the morning giving physical examinations to the children. Mothers who were free to assist were scheduled to help in the school regularly. In the spring of the first year a graduate in kindergarten work was added to the staff, full time. The original enrollment was later increased to

---

[3] *The Co-operative Nursery School,* pp. 9 ff. Ethel Peiffer Hawes and Dorothea Beach. Bulletin, Smith College, Northampton, Mass., 1928.

twenty-five children. Children from two to four years of age formed one group; those from four to five years formed another.

The organization of this co-operative nursery school is believed to be unique. It illustrates a practical type of organization which should be less expensive than the ordinary nursery school. It takes into consideration parent education as a part of the larger educational scheme.

In the two co-operative nursery schools discussed above, opportunity for securing an integrated experience for the child, one that links the home to the school and the school to the home, has been provided in different ways, with results that appear to be helpful both to the child and to the parent. The policy of combining the efforts of parent and teacher in directing the educative processes of the child has also appeared at the elementary and secondary levels in many schools.

PURPOSE OF THIS STUDY

The present study attempts to probe the practices used by mothers in situations arising in a co-operative nursery school where the activities were in many respects similar to those in the home, and it also endeavors to show the activities of the children under observation in the same situations. No attempt is made, however, to explain the causal sequences occurring in these situations. Nevertheless, general trends in the behavior of both mothers and children are shown in the results of the study, and these are elaborated. The records studied concern a small group of mothers who engaged in a narrow range of nursery school activities; but the data are objective and are compiled from actual records of the conduct of both mothers and children in the nursery school.

The specific purpose of this study was to investigate the following practices of mothers and the activities of children in a co-operative nursery school:

1. Practices used by mothers in the situations observed.

2. Activities of a child or of children in situations in which the mother participated.

3. Activities of a child or of children in situations in which the mother did not participate.

4. Language used by mothers in guiding the children in the situations under observation.

No information was available as to the practices used by the children's parents or by maids employed in the home. The attempt to discover the nature of the practices of the parents in family life has been made by other investigators, but the paucity of the material secured has precluded any accurate conclusions. Because of the difficulty of obtaining reliable data, the importance of the practices used by parents in home situations has not been considered in the present study.

Chapter II
SOURCES OF DATA

THIS study was undertaken to determine the practices used by mothers in dealing with problems of child guidance, and to study the activities of children in a co-operative nursery school. The investigator sought to obtain objective data showing the practices of the mothers and the behavior of the children in situations comparable to those of everyday occurrence in the home. The opportunity to secure such data was provided when the experimenter was selected by a group of parents to direct a co-operative nursery school which they had organized and planned to carry on in the home of one of the members of the group. The purposes of the parents in organizing such a school were to provide supervised social contacts for their children at less expense than was possible in other nursery schools in the city, and to develop in themselves greater insight into the behavior problems of their children in order to improve their technique in the solution of these problems.

The Co-operative Nursery School consisted of two large rooms and two gardens. The rooms were furnished to provide for rest periods and meals and had such equipment as paints, crayons, clay, books, and a victrola for indoor activities. The two gardens used by the children contained a jungle gym, one large sandbox, a seesaw, a fish pond, and a toy house, as well as numerous motor toys. Blocks and packing boxes of various sizes were available for use in play. During the year the children received gifts of pets, including a rabbit, white mice, goldfish, an alligator, a dog, and a kitten.

Fees assessed by the parents were used to meet the expenses of maintenance and to purchase additional play equipment as it was needed. This money was budgeted by a committee and the budget included all operating expenses.

The Co-operative Nursery School opened October 3, 1931, and continued in session for eight consecutive months, closing May

31, 1932. During these eight months two vacation periods were provided: two weeks at Christmas and one week preceding Easter Sunday. The school was in session from 8:45 to 11:45 a. m., five days each week, from Monday to Friday, inclusive.

SUBJECTS OF THE STUDY

The Parents. Eleven mothers participated in the activities of the school. One mother, whose professional interests required her presence when the school was in session, was unable to act as assistant but co-operated with the school in other ways. Each of the eleven mothers in turn helped with the Nursery School, by serving as an assistant to the experimenter for one week at a time according to a definite schedule. In the original group ten mothers enrolled one child each in the school and two mothers enrolled two children each.

The parents, several of whom had similar professional interests, were from similar social and cultural levels. They were, for the most part, college-trained people who were pursuing some vocational or avocational activity.

Among the fathers, there were five who practiced different branches of specialized medicine; two were architects; one was a broker; one, a bond salesman; one, an investment banker; one, a manufacturer; and one, a metallurgical engineer, who was temporarily working outside his profession in the employ of a large retail department store. The yearly incomes of these men ranged from $3,000 to $15,000.

The mothers, by virtue of their training or vocations, represented a variety of interests. One mother had a Master of Arts degree, and five had Bachelor of Arts degrees from accredited institutions; two had attended college but held no degrees; two had attended finishing schools; and one, a graduate nurse, had attended college for one year. Four mothers were following careers independent of their husbands' careers, while one was acting as her husband's assistant. Without exception, a primary concern of all the mothers was child training; and the seven mothers who were not engaged in vocational activity outside the home had each taken organized courses dealing with problems of child welfare.

The twelve mothers who either co-operated or participated with the experimenter in the activities of the Nursery School ranged in age from twenty-five to thirty-five years. They showed no signs of illness, and in only one instance was an absence from duty in the Nursery School caused by illness. No individual in the group had received any training in the science and art involved in homemaking. As has been mentioned, one mother was a graduate nurse, a training which approximates in some respects that given homemakers.

The Children. Twelve children were enrolled in the original group. Two children were withdrawn on the first of February to accompany their parents on a trip abroad. These vacancies were immediately filled from a list of applicants. Another child was withdrawn during April for a month's vacation with her parents. In this instance, also, a substitution was made in the group. The mother who was unable to participate in the nursery school activities because of professional interests enrolled another child in the school. When the child on temporary leave returned, her substitute was allowed to remain until the close of school, but no observations or records were made of the substitute's activity because of her irregular attendance. Of the fifteen children, then, nine attended for eight calendar months, four for six months, one for seven months, and one for two months. Records were made of the activities of fourteen children.

Preceding their entrance into the Nursery School, the children were examined by their family physicians. The reports showed that the children were in good health and had no physical defects. Each child was given the Schick test and diphtheria inoculations. The only illnesses occurring during the eight months were colds. The children were required to remain away from school during the illness, and for five days after any visible signs of a cold, such as irritated throat or discharge from the nose, had disappeared. The children's weights and heights corresponded very closely to the weight and height of standards for children of their age. Two children were overweight by only a few pounds. One boy in the group showed poor muscular co-ordination which was diagnosed by the family physician not as an abnormality but as underdevelopment caused by a lack of opportunity to walk, run, jump, and climb, accompanied by a seeming lack of interest in such activities.

The children in the school group ranged in age from eighteen months to four years. The group included two children at the eighteen months' level; seven, two years old; three, three years old; and two, four years old. The ages were computed from the first of October of the school year. A child was placed in the age group which corresponded to his last birthday if six months had not expired since that date; otherwise, he was included in the age group above.

Each of the children had both parents living in the home. Six of the children who joined the Nursery School during the year were the only children in the family; five belonged to families in which there were two children; and three were members of families in which there were three children.

Each child had a separate room from that of the adults in the family, except one child who shared the bedroom of her parents. One brother and sister occupied the same room, and two brothers also shared one room. Each home was attractively furnished and conveniently arranged, with adequate space, ventilation; and lighting.

NATURE OF THE DATA

The data that were obtained consisted of stenographic records made by an observer of the activities of the eleven mothers and the fourteen children as they participated in the activities of the Nursery School. The records were originally made in shorthand by a trained stenographer who had had previous experience in making records of children's activities, and who was designated as the observer. The observer transcribed immediately the notes made at school and brought the records to the experimenter on the following morning. A record was made of the activities of a particular mother or child assigned to the observer for observation, describing the overt behavior exhibited by each as expressed by movements, by the choice and use of equipment, and by any verbalization that took place. Records were also made of the activities of those children in the group who made contacts with the mother or the child under observation during the period.[1]

The records of the children covered three-hour periods, the length of the daily session of the Nursery School. The entire observation period for each child consisted of three three-hour periods, representing a total of nine hours. The nine hours included one three-hour period before the child's mother had acted as assistant in the Nursery School, one three-hour period at the time the child's mother was assisting in the school, and a final observation of three hours when another mother was acting as assistant. No record was made of a child's activities until he had been in the Nursery School a minimum of two weeks. No child was observed after any absence from school until a week had passed. For example, if a child had been in school two weeks and then was absent, he was not observed until a week after his return to school.

The time allowed for observation of each mother was three three-hour periods, or a total of nine hours. The observation periods of each mother included one three-hour period on Monday, the first day she participated as assistant in the Nursery School, and one period of three hours on both Wednesday and Thursday of the same week, when she also acted as assistant.

The schedule given below shows the distribution of observation periods for the five days.

SCHEDULE SHOWING DISTRIBUTION OF OBSERVATION PERIODS

	Monday	Tuesday	Wednesday	Thursday	Friday
Child		3 hours			Reserved for the child whose mother was next assistant in
Mother....	3 hours		3 hours	3 hours	the Nursery School.

[1] The term "contact," as employed in this study, is defined as a verbal or physical exchange between mother and child, or between child and child.

Several changes in observation plans of the mothers' practices were unavoidable. The time which was set for the mothers to act as assistants and to be observed was changed in two instances. On the dates when Mothers IX and IV were scheduled for observation, the former's two children and the latter's child were absent from school because of colds; they were therefore asked to change observation time with another mother who had not been observed. This arrangement made it imperative for the observer to make records for the final observations on three children one week and four children the next week. Mother VI did not act as assistant in the Nursery School as scheduled, but, after an unavoidable delay, was observed at another time in the schedule. In other words, her records followed the plan of observation mapped out for other mothers, but the date for making the record was changed. Mother V spent much time in and out of the Nursery School before her record was made. She was a relative of the family in whose home the Nursery School was held. Her concern was to acquaint the experimenter and assistants with the location of equipment and supplies, but she spent no consecutive time observing the activities of either mothers or children before her record was made. It is entirely possible, however, that Mother V overheard instruction and suggestions made to the children which might have influenced some of her practices in the Nursery School.

One limitation in this study which affected the records of the children was the variation in time that elapsed before the child was assigned for observation. A few of the records show behavior that was no doubt the result of lack of orientation to the group and to the Nursery School environment. On the other hand, the children who were observed later in the term had the advantage of a longer period of orientation.

METHODS OF SECURING DATA

An observer was introduced to the parents as a stenographer employed by the experimenter to make records of the children's behavior in the school. This partial explanation was given the parents by the experimenter so that the mothers would not be embarrassed in the presence of either the observer or the experimenter.[2]

Experience of the Observer. The observer had had three years' experience at the Child Development Institute, Teachers College, Columbia University, in recording for scientific study the behavior exhibited and the language used by slightly older children than those who were to compose the Nursery School group to be studied. In order to qualify more satisfactorily and to get experience in noting and recording the verbalization of children of approximately the age to be studied, however, she spent five three-hour practice periods making records in the Nursery School at the Child Development Institute, where it was thought the environment would be similar to that which would be established in the Co-operative Nursery School used in this study.

Accuracy of the Observer Tested.[3] Following the practice period at the Institute, the reliability of the observer was checked by a second observer who had also participated in previous studies made at the Child Development Institute. The two observers made simultaneous records of the activities of one child selected from the group. The sample record showing the agreements and disagreements between the two observers is given below. The body of the text, with the exception of the parentheses, shows the agreements. The parentheses indicate disagreements in observation, and the nature of these discrepancies is stated under the column headings "Observer A" and "Observer B," respectively. These records were made of the activities of B, one of the youngest children in the group.

---

[2] When she was employed, the experimenter had explained to the parents that she was interested in making a study of the individual child's behavior in the Nursery School and was at that time given permission by the parents to make this study.

[3] The method used in testing the accuracy of the observers was the method described in Arrington's study, *Interrelations in the Behavior of Young Children.* This method is the percentage analysis of agreement between observers in the recording of activities within five-second intervals. The percentage of agreement between observers represents the quotient obtained when the value representing the number of items in each observer's record agreeing with items in the other observer's record is divided by this value plus disagreements.

EXCERPT FROM CHILD "B'S" RECORD

Activities Found in the Record of the Two Observers

Observer A		*Observer B*

¹(Dumps blocks out of wheel-barrow)
²(Kicks)

Children in play yard. B piles blocks into wheelbarrow, pushes wheelbarrow into next yard (1), runs around the yard pushing empty wheelbarrow— starts to push wheelbarrow down board. J (2) wheelbarrow and says, "B, get out of the way." B pulls wheelbarrow back, runs around yard pushing wheel-barrow then trips and falls, gets up again, continues pushing wheelbarrow, slips and falls on board, stands up— pushing wheelbarrow again, picks up brick, puts brick in wheelbarrow, lifts wheelbarrow onto slide. Teacher says, "Take your wheelbarrow off the slide, B." B moves wheelbarrow, throws it down, goes into the garden, picks up stick, carries stick on shoulder, and says, "Here's the soldier, here's the soldier"—follows K and E who are marching around the yard. B stops marching, scrapes sand with stick, climbs up jungle gym ladder and says, "Up the ladder—(3)." B climbs down the ladder, runs to J. (4) and B says, "I had it first." J says, "No, this goes into the cupboard, because everybody falls on it."

¹(Throws blocks out of wheel-barrow)
²(Pushes at)

³("I do this")
⁴(B grabs tricycle)

³("I go like this")
⁴(J grabs tricycle)

B sits on K.K. and rides a few feet, leaves K.K. and goes to teacher and says, "Teacher, get bunny out." B goes to fish pond, teacher says, "B, B, this way; you can see from here." Teacher takes bunny out of cage and says, "B, get something for Peter to ride in." Mother IV says to B, "B, do you have to go to the bathroom?" B says, "No, I don't." Teacher puts bunny in carriage and B holds the carriage handle. J comes over to B and

Observer A		*Observer B*
[5](Takes hold of handle)	J (5). B says, "No, mine." Q comes over and (6). B goes away with the carriage.	[5](Takes handle away from B)
[6](B pushes Q)		[6](Q pushes B)
	G says, "B." B looks at G, B leaves carriage. G calls, "B, come get your carriage." B sits on step between K and D. B holds "Tiddly Winks" (doll) in hand. D says, "I want that." B runs around the yard and D follows him. D sits down beside B on fence. Then both run back to steps and sit down. D (7) "Tiddly Winks"; B cries	
[7](Grabs)		[7](B gives D "Tiddly Winks")
	and says, "I had that first." B goes to tricycle and says, "I want that." K says, "That's E's." B goes to tool shed, pulls doors open, looks in, then	
[8](B says, "I make a tower")	goes to blocks. (8) B piles up blocks. Teacher says, "B, there are many more blocks over there in the other yard, if	[8](B begins playing with blocks)
[9](B says, "I pick them up")	you need more." (9)	[9](B begins picking up blocks)
	Teacher says, "I'll help you. Carry them carefully, B." B says, "I want another one, over there." B plays with blocks, pulls sack over his head, piles up blocks, blocks fall over, and B leaves blocks. Picks up truck, carries truck	
[10](B says something)	up slide, then B (10), carries truck up board again and pushes it down.	[10](B says to D, "Watch out for . . .")
[11](Goes to carriage)	B (11), B falls down, stands up, and goes to toy house. (12) and strikes dog.	[11](Leaves out)
[12](Bends over)	Runs to wheelbarrow, pulls wheelbarrow, runs to table for tomato juice.	[12](Stoops down)

After obtaining the complete composite record, a portion of which is reproduced above, the experimenter checked Observer A's record against Observer B's record for sequence of behavior recorded, number of times the child pursued a new interest, any changes that occurred in the direction in which the activity developed, and for a description of what the child did in the development of his interests, including the language he used. These records, as checked by the experimenter, show, first, that the sequence of the child's activity was agreed upon by the two observers; and, second, that certain agreements and disagreements existed. Closer examination of the two records shows agreement upon both the sequence of the activities and the large activities observed. The disagreements occur in descriptions of the lesser activities, such as changes in directions of the interests pursued, and the methods used in following through the interests.

To determine further the accuracy of Observer A, the experimenter checked the records for total number of children's activities observed.[4] The total number similarly recorded by each of the two observers was 324. In addition, Observer B recorded twenty items on which A did not show agreement, and Observer A recorded twenty-five items on which B did not show agreement. Percentages of agreement as to the occurrences of activities based upon the two records made simultaneously by Observer A and Observer B of the children's activities, the agreements shown in Observer A's record when analyzed, and the percentage of agreement computed according to Arrington's method, were 90 per cent.

To check the accuracy of Observer A in making records of the mothers' activities[5] in the Nursery School, Observer B was

[4] The term "activities" is used here to describe the overt behavior of the children in the solution of problems or the development of interests. Overt behavior is shown in the records of descriptions of changes in the direction of behavior; of descriptions of methods used and changes in method; of descriptions of the naming and using of play materials, play equipment, or equipment of any nature. Descriptions of overt behavior as shown by the activities of the child were checked and the total absence or lack of complete agreement in the description was counted as a disagreement in the record.

[5] The term "activities" is here used to describe the overt behavior of the mothers in the solution of problems or in the development of interests. Overt behavior is shown in the records by descriptions of changes in the direction of behavior; by descriptions of the naming and using of play materials, play equipment, or equipment of any nature; and by descriptions of methods used and of changes in method. The descriptions of overt behavior as shown by the activities were checked, and the total absence or complete lack of agreement in the descriptions was counted as a disagreement in the records.

again introduced into the situation. Both observers made simultaneous records of the activities and practices of Mother VIII.[6] These records were checked by the experimenter to determine agreements in describing the activities of both mother and child. An excerpt from the resultant composite record of Mother VIII is given below to show agreements and disagreements. The two observers, it was found, agreed upon the sequence of activities and upon the larger activities, but disagreed upon some of the minor activities. There were ten instances where the language record of the mother did not show agreement in the two records. The total number of mothers' activities noted by both Observer A and Observer B was 285. Observer A failed to agree with B's description of seventeen activities, and Observer B failed to agree with Observer A in the description of twenty-three activities. Five of the activities in Observer A's records which failed to agree with Observer B's description were activities in which the language of the mother was involved; and nine of the activities in B's records which showed disagreements with A were activities in which the mother spoke to the child. Other disagreements were scattered throughout the records.[7] The results of the checking of the two records show an agreement between the two observers of 92 per cent.

Portions of two observations are also included to indicate the nature of the records from which the data of this study are taken. The first sample given on page 26 is a part of the record made of J's activities during one three-hour period; the second is a portion of the record of Mother X's activities during her three-hour assistantship in the Nursery School.

[6] Mother VIII served two weeks in succession at the beginning of the year, and a second observer was used in the second week to check the accuracy of Observer A in making records of this mother's activities as she participated in the Nursery School.

[7] Seventy-five per cent of the disagreements occurred either in the toileting situation or in preparation for rest. The bathrooms were very small and the observers were forced to remain outside while making the records, which fact probably accounts for the large percentage of disagreements in describing the bathroom activities.

An Excerpt from Mother VIII's Record

Activities Found in the Records of the Two Observers

Observer A		Observer B
	H goes to the bathroom crying. Mother says, "Stand up on the box." He stands up on the box and Mother says, "Now go to the bathroom. That's fine —now step down. Pull up your trousers." H pulls at pants. Mother says, "Now pull up the zipper—pull hard. I	
¹(Mother holds buttonhole and helps H push button)	will help you fasten this." (1) Mother says, "Now flush the toilet, will you, please?" "Do you know where it is? Just push that string back there."	¹(Mother fastens H's pants)
²(Mother goes into yard and speaks to C)	Mother goes into yard. (2) C walks into the house and goes to bathroom and sits on toilet fully dressed. Mother says, "Don't you think you had better pull your clothes down first? Suppose you get down and step outside. We are going to let D go first—she is younger." C goes out of the bathroom and Mother says to D, "Suppose you stand here and we will pull your things down." Mother unfastens D's panties and lifts her onto the toilet seat and steps out of the bathroom. Mother says, "Do you like the nice donkey?" Mother goes back to D and says, "Have you finished?" D says something and Mother says, "Slip down on the floor." D slips down—Mother says, "Can you pull up your trousers?" D pulls and Mother says, "That's fine; take hold of your leggings here in front and pull them up." D pulls and Mother fastens the leggings. Mother says, "Now go into the yard." D goes into the yard. Mother unfastens C's panties, and lifts her onto the toilet seat. Mother says, "Now go to the bathroom and tell me when you have finished." Mother waits a few minutes and says, "Hurry	²(Mother says, "It is time to go to the bathroom")

Observer A		Observer B

up, C." Mother leaves the bathroom. C says, "I am through." Mother lifts C off toilet, fastens clothes, and C goes out into the yard.

Mother goes into play yard, speaks to teacher, and goes into next yard and stands beside C, who is on the ladder. C goes off ladder, mother sits down and watches the children. K jumps in a box and breaks the top in. Mother says, "Just a minute, K. Sit on the box."

³("Don't jump on box")   Mother says to K, "Be careful." (3) Then Mother goes over to chair and sits down. K turns around on swing and starts swinging backward. Mother says, "K, you had better swing the other way, then if you fall you will land

⁴(J grabs swing and tries to get on)   on the mat." (4) Mother says, "K had it. Ask K for it." J says to K, "Can I have it?" K says, "Please." J repeats "please" and K walks away.   ⁴(J tries to get on swing when K stands up)

J says, "Will you read to us after we have tomato juice?" Mother walks away. Mother takes B and H by the hand. They go upstairs. Mother walks

⁵(Mother takes off B's sweater and leggings)   up the stairs behind them. (5) The maid comes in and takes B to rest. Mother takes off H's clothes. H cries and goes into bathroom and stands on basin steps. Mother turns on the water and hands H a piece of soap and says, "Do we use the beautiful green soap?" H takes the soap and Mother washes H's hands and face. Mother says, "Get   ⁵(Mother helps B take off his sweater and leggings)

⁶("We will dry your hands." Mother dries his hands and face)   down, H." (6) H steps down.   ⁶(H dries his hands and face. "Now, I think we will go to the bathroom before you rest")

AN EXCERPT FROM MOTHER VIII'S RECORD (*Continued*)

Observer A		Observer B
7(Changes H's shirt)	Mother gets dry pants. Mother holds pants and H steps into them. Mother (7)	7("We will put dry clothes on you." Mother puts shirt over H's head, and H puts arms through armhole)

OBSERVATION OF J (GIRL)

November 15, 1932

Age: 4 years

Recorder: A. M. B.

Assistant: J's mother (Mother VIII)

M—Mother

T—Teacher

J—Child under observation

Other letters—individual children

9:00.—Children play in yard. J sits on the tricycle and rides to M. J says, "Look at the puppy. He is going to bite your fur, isn't he?" J gets off tricycle, goes into next yard, and pushes doll carriage around yard. Pushes carriage to steps, holds handle and lets carriage slowly down steps. B runs over to carriage, holds carriage, and J says, "No, B, don't." B walks away and J pushes carriage over to M and says, "Sit down with me, Mummy." M walks over to another chair and sits down. J picks up a stool and follows M, and says, "D is cute, isn't she?" Then J opens out stool and sits on it, beside M. M gets up and J turns around on stool and holds a shovel which was sticking out of sand box. Then J gets up from stool and carries stool in one hand and pushes the carriage with the other hand. J says to M, "What are you going to do?" and follows M to door. J goes in house, comes out again, brings a book, and says, "Look, Mummy, this is 'Sing a Song of Sixpence.'" I takes the doll out of the carriage and H yells, "No!" and grabs the doll back and puts it into the carriage. T says, "Do you want to bring your carriage up here?" J says, "No," and T says, "You would have more room in the other yard." M sits on box. J follows M, opens out stool, and sits on it beside M and looks at book.

9:15.—J puts book in carriage. G comes over and pulls carriage.

J says, "No, I had this first," and pulls at the handle. G says, "Let me have it." J turns to M and says, "I had it first, Mummy." M comes over and says, "J, remember yesterday, we said the carriage was here for everybody. I think it would be nice to let G have it for awhile." J then walks away and leaves the carriage. G says, "I want the doll." J says, "You go and get another doll upstairs." J puts the doll in the wagon and covers it with a doll cover. J goes over to M and says, "G is going to get another doll." M says, "I think it would have been nicer if you did, don't you?" M sits on chair and J walks over and kneels down beside M and says, "See what I am going to do, Mummy. Look, I put the clown doll in the basket, Mummy." J stands up, walks over to T and says, "See what I did. I put the clown doll in the basket." Then G comes and picks up the clown from the basket and runs into the house. J follows G into the house and T comes over to the door and calls, "This way, J. Out here." J says something and goes upstairs. J comes out of house, walks over to M and says, "I can't find it, Mummy," and leans against M. J runs over to slide, steps on box, slides down head first on her stomach. J gets up at bottom of slide and says, "I slid down on my stomach." J runs back to box and steps up and says, "You come after me, L." J slides down again on stomach, then runs back again, steps up again, and G says, "My turn first." J says, "No, it's my turn before G." J pushes G aside and slides down again on her stomach. J runs back and says, "I am going to go down this way." She lies on her stomach and slides down, feet first.

9:30.—J runs over to box of Kleenex, takes one out of the box, and T says, "No, give it to L." J says, "I want one," and T says, "No, you don't need one." Then J walks over to doll carriage, picks up a clown doll, and G says, "No, that's mine. Don't touch that," and pulls at the doll. J places doll in carriage again and G says, "Get a doll upstairs." J goes into house and brings out a doll, walks over to M, and says, "Will you fasten this, Mummy, please?" She hands doll to M and M fastens the ribbon. G comes over and grabs the doll. M says, "G, I think J went upstairs for this dolly; you might ask her for it later." J sits on a box and puts on doll's dress. J says, "Where's the pillow?" and T says, "There was one in the small basket. Where's the basket?" J says, "Mummy is going to bring it down." D stands beside carriage. J goes over, picks up doll from carriage and drops it on ground, then puts her doll in carriage and covers it up and says, "There's my doll now." G comes over and says, "That's my dolly." J says, "No, I got this dolly. You get the other. The puppy took the other." T comes over and J says, "The puppy took her doll and ran away with it." T says, "How did the puppy get it?" J says,

"I don't know. He took it out of the carriage." T says, "The puppy couldn't reach up in the carriage. You see, it's too high. Where did the puppy get the doll?" J says, "It was on the ground." T says, "How did it get on the ground?" J says, "Somebody put it there." J looks into next yard and cries, "Oh, there's the dolly. The puppy has it." T goes into next yard and brings doll back.

OBSERVATION OF MOTHER X (P's MOTHER)

April 13, 1933

Recorder: A. M. B.   M—Mother

Children present: P, Mother X's child, Q, K, G, C, J, E, B, D, A, L, F

9:00.—Children in play yard. P sits in sandbox, digs; gets up and walks around yard, carries small roller coaster. M says to P, "Do you want to pull D? I will hold this for you." M takes coaster and P starts to pull. D steps out.

9:15.—P sits in wagon and M pulls wagon. P gets out of wagon, pulls wagon herself. Q takes toy out of wagon. P cries and M says, "Well, go and take it back. Don't cry. She took it from you. You go and take it away from her." P runs after Q and takes toy. P puts toy in wagon and pulls wagon around yard.

9:30.—P picks up carrots from ground and puts them in carriage near rabbit. P holds wagon handle and B tries to get past. M says, "P, let go." P lets go the handle. B walks past and P grabs handle again and holds wagon. P leaves wagon and picks up bag of vegetables for rabbit and holds carriage. M says, "Come on, P. Give D a ride." P says, "No." M says, "Oh, yes; she gave you a ride." P says to D, "You want a ride?" D pushes wagon, then walks away. P holds carriage handle and watches F, who is behind house doors. K rides to P on kiddie kar and says, "P, you sit on the back here." Q goes to carriage and takes hold of handle. P cries and M says, "P, listen to me. Don't cry. If somebody takes something away from you, take it back."

9:45.—P goes to house door and says, "I want to come in." K says, "No." M says, "Let everybody come in. Move over. Here, P, you get in there." P goes behind door and stands. Other children leave and P stands by herself behind the doors and pushes them open and closes them and talks to herself quietly. M says, "What's the matter? Do you want to get out?" P climbs up on door and M says, "Here, wait a minute." M opens door and P says, "No," and fastens door again. M walks away. P cries and M goes right back to her and says, "The children are going to look for Easter eggs." P comes out from behind door and goes to sandbox, stands at bench and brushes sand with hands, then picks up spoon and scrapes sand into pile on bench. P goes to toy house and cries and says, "Let me in." C says, "No, P, you can't come in." P goes back to sandbox, holds out hand to Q and says, "I want it. I want it." G comes to P and says, "I want to play with doll." P cries and moves away.

SUMMARY

1. The purpose of the investigator in making this study was to collect and analyze objective data showing the practices of mothers and the activities of children in a nursery school where conditions were somewhat comparable to everyday conditions in the home.

2. The mothers who participated in this experiment belonged to the professional class, and were above the average in cultural background and socio-economic status. Their purposes in organizing a nursery school were (1) to provide supervised social contacts for their children in an environment less expensive than that of any nursery school available in their section of the city, and (2) to develop greater insight into the behavior problems of children in order to improve their own techniques in the solution of these problems.

3. This Co-operative Nursery School, which was held in the home of one of the parents, included twelve mothers whose ages ranged from twenty-five to thirty-five years, and fourteen children from eighteen months to four years of age.

4. Each mother, except one who was employed, assisted the experimenter, according to schedule, for a week. An experienced observer was employed to make stenographic records of the activities of both mothers and children. These records covered three three-hour periods, or a total of nine hours, for each child and for each of the eleven mothers who acted as assistants. The records of each child covered two observation periods when his mother was absent, and one when she was present. The mother's observation schedule was arranged so that records of her activities and practices were made the first week she acted as assistant.

5. Excerpts from two records of a child, each made simultaneously by two observers disclosed an agreement of 90 per cent as to the activities the observers witnessed. Excerpts from the records of a mother also made simultaneously by the same observers likewise showed minor disagreements. As in the case of the child's records, both observers agreed in most of the instances recorded, the percentage of agreement being 92.

Chapter III

DISCUSSION OF MOTHERS' PRACTICES USED IN DIRECTING CHILDREN'S ACTIVITIES

ANALYSIS OF MOTHERS' PRACTICES

THE experimenter arbitrarily selected one record of the activities of each of the eleven mothers and fourteen children in order to expedite the study of similarities of the mothers' practices and similarities of the children's activities in the same situations. Nine first-day, seven second-day, and nine third-day records of mothers and children were used in setting up tentative classifications for the study of the practices of the mothers and the activities of the children. The remaining twenty-two records of the mothers' practices and the twenty-eight unused records of the children's activities were employed in the clarification and revision of the classifications used in the study of the mothers' practices and the children's activities. The eleven records of the mothers' practices and the records of the fourteen children's activities showed certain similarities and, on the basis of these similarities, could be classified into more comprehensive groups. Each large group included those activities through which the mother and the child tried to solve a problem or develop an interest. These large units of activities the experimenter chose to call "situations." A situation, then, as the term is used in this study, is composed of activities which involve both mother and child and which are directed toward the solution of a problem or the development of an interest. A situation was understood to begin when the mother first spoke to the child of an activity or gave him a physical stimulus to which he responded, or vice versa. A situation was considered closed and a new activity started when the mother or child responded to a new verbal or physical stimulus, differing in character from the previous one.

The experimenter and the observer analyzed the original records for situations and each found the same number, a total of 221. A third person, designated in the discussion as the "checker," was introduced into the situation to work with the observer and the experimenter in accurately analyzing the data. When the observer and the checker analyzed the original records for situations and their results were compared with those found when the checker and the experimenter analyzed the same records, it was discovered that the observer had differed with the experimenter twenty-four times and the experimenter had differed with the observer twenty times as to the beginning and the conclusion of a situation. These discrepancies were studied, and it was found that the experimenter and the checker agreed on the activities inherent in the solution of the problem and in the development of an interest, but disagreed on those activities of the mothers and children which were not directed toward solving a problem or forming an interest. These disagreements were shown in the classification of such activities as the following: (1) those which described going to or coming from the place where a problem had been solved; (2) those which occurred while the participants in a situation were preparing for the solution of a problem or the development of an interest; and (3) those which followed the solution of a problem or the development of an interest and apparently were not vitally related to the preceding or following activities. The experimenter's record showed an agreement of 91 per cent with the assistant's in determining the activities of mother and children which were to be included in the large units of activity, or situations. In cases where there was any disagreement, the observer and the experimenter went over the situations together and determined the activity which had begun and ended a situation.

Next, the records of each of the mothers and children were studied to determine the similarities in activities engaged in by the group of mothers. Each type of practice was defined and then the definitions were clarified by describing the practices in greater detail and by pointing out those activities which were used in determining the classification. This regrouping of the mothers' practices involved changes in the classification: (1) in descriptions of what the mother did in order to eliminate any interepretation of her purpose, (2) in the distribution and reclassification of the methods used, and (3) in the descriptions of certain activities of the mothers and children which had determined the classification of a particular practice.

From a study of the similarities in the activities engaged in by the mothers, it was found that these activities could be grouped into thirteen classifications, each of which revealed in a general way the practices of the mothers in directing the children in following through an interest or in solving a problem. These thirteen large units of activity were in turn analyzed in order to discover the *methods* used by the mothers in carrying out the practices in question, and the following classification of methods was developed. Each classification is illustrated by an example taken from the original record.

CLASSIFICATION OF METHODS BASED ON SIMILARI- TIES BETWEEN MOTHERS' PRACTICES

The following thirteen definitions explain the methods employed by the mothers. The classifications used in the study of the mothers' practices, the children's activities, and the children's behavior, together with the category used in grouping the situations, were first defined and presented to a seminar group at the Child Development Institute, Teachers College, Columbia University. Suggestions and recommendations were made by members of the seminar to the experimenter, who further clarified the definitions by describing the practices more in detail and adding explanations and pointing out activities which illustrated the meaning of the classifications.

1. *Seeks Information.* This classification includes those methods used by the mother when securing information from the child by probing his knowledge, interest, or desire.[1] The following questions illustrate four situations in which the mother is seeking information:

[1] The classification, "Question Group," included situations in which the mother waited for a verbal response from the child, and the child's answer had a subsequent effect upon the mother's activities. Other questions were classified under several other headings.

a) Questions child's need.

Situation: Mother II says to B, "Do you want to get on the toilet?" B says, "I can't." Mother says, "All right, but remember that you had wet pants yesterday."

b) Questions child for information.

Situation: Mother II picks up toys in the yard—stoops down and kisses Q. D and B both hold tricycle. Mother says, "Who had it?" B says, "It's mine." D cries. Mother says, "I am sure B had it first."

c) Questions whether or not child is able to do task.

Situation: Mother II says, "Can you fasten this, or shall I do it?" (referring to garter). C says, "I don't know how to do it. I am so little. When I am big I will know how to do it." Mother fastens garter and puts C's rubbers on—then both go downstairs.

d) Questions child's interest.

Situation: Mother VI dances a bit and says. "Doesn't anybody want to dance?" J says, "You do it." Mother says, "I just wanted to get you started."

2. Offers Explanation. This classification includes those methods used by the mother when she explains something of which she deems the child either is ignorant or has imperfect knowledge. The explanation requires such activities of the mother as are necessary to give the child a conception of the ideas involved. This method[2] is used by the mother when she (*a*) explains equipment or use of equipment to the child, (*b*) explains an activity or term, or (*c*) demonstrates how a thing is done by showing the various steps, and also the basis for the procedure.

c) Situation: Mother I says to G, "G, let me show you how to use the scissors. Put them on your hand like this. Then hold your picture like this. Cut very slowly around the edge of your picture. Now put the scissors on your hand and I will help you cut this one out."

3. Diverts Attention. Diverts Attention embraces those methods employed by the mother to deflect the child's attention from an

[2] Only one illustration under each classification is necessary to give the reader an idea of the nature of the situations in each classification. The situation used is identified in each case by the small letters that relate it to the particular practice illustrated.

undesirable activity or interest in order to direct it toward a more desirable one. For example, the mother (*a*) may remind the child of a former interest or activity or may call attention to a new activity, or (*b*) may offer a substitute activity.

a) Situation: Mother II lifts D on a chair and says, "Let's see what's wrong." Mother takes off shoe and sock, then says, "Is your foot cold?" D cries. Mother says, "We will put your sock back on again and your shoe." Mother puts sock and shoe back on again and says, "Now we will go back to the kiddie kar." D stops crying and goes into the yard.

4. *Urges*. The activities of the mother which tend to push the child into an activity, to resume an activity that has been delayed, or to conclude an activity are included in this classification.[3] The mother may motivate the situation by (*a*) using words that imply speed, (*b*) calling attention to consideration for others, (*c*) reminding child of activity that can be resumed, or (*d*) suggesting competition.

(*c*) Situation: Mother VIII walks over to B and says, "B, go to the bathroom." B says, "No," and walks away from mother. Mother follows and says, "Come to the bathroom, then you can come right out again. It won't take long." B holds mother's hand and they go into the bathroom.

5. *Directs*. This classification includes those activities of the mother which indicate an authoritative purpose, and in which specific directions are given as to how to perform an act or a series of acts, with no recourse open to the child short of outright disobedience. The mother may (*a*) say that the equipment belongs to the child, (*b*) tell the child to place the toy, equipment, or clothes in a certain place or in a certain way, or give the child the order of a routine, (*c*) tell the child to co-operate or to share in the use of equipment, (*d*) point out equipment to the child, (*e*) guide the child physically, by the hand or by taking hold of his shoulders, (*f*) give the child permission or refuse his request, (*g*) omit the task from the routine, or (*h*) do the task for the child.

---

[3] *Urges* differs from *forces* in that the activities of the child give no evidence of opposition to the mother's activities. The child's activities are characterized by dawdling and interest detached from the problem or duty to be carried out.

(*c*) Situation: K sits on one end of the seesaw, Mother VII stands near. L stands near K watching him. Mother VII says to L, "You get on the other end of the seesaw and you can seesaw with K." L runs to opposite end of board from K and sits down on board.

6. *Encourages.*[4] This classification embraces methods used by the mother to give the child courage in an activity where he has hesitated either to begin or to complete a problem which offered difficulties. The mother may use one of the following methods: (*a*) share activity with the child, (*b*) show child how to manipulate equipment, (*c*) call attention to order in the solution of the problem, or (*d*) express a willingness to co-operate.

d) Situation: Mother VI walks to next yard and watches F and C, who are behind the gate. F says, "I want to get out." Mother says, "Can I help you?" "Here, push it off this, now take it off—. Here, do you want to come out, F?" F comes out and mother says, "Say 'thank you' to C."

7. *Impedes.*[5] *Impedes* describes activities of the mother which interfere with the progress of the child's plan. For example, the mother may (*a*) use physical interference, (*b*) refuse child equipment or privilege, (*c*) remind child of another person's directions or orders, (*d*) use verbal interference, or (*e*) remind child of previous threat or threaten child with punishment.

a) Situation: J throws sand into the sandbox. Mother V comes over to the sandbox and takes J by the hands. J looks at mother, gets out of the sandbox, and dusts her coat off. Mother walks a few feet away, continues to watch J.

[4] Children in situations classified under this heading showed indecision in their activities and often were thwarted by too complicated and difficult duties. This was shown by hesitation and repeated trials with little or no success. The activities of the children in these cases showed no dawdling, detached interest, or resentment overtly expressed.

[5] Situations were classified under *impedes* when the progress of the child's activities was judged as unacceptable and unsatisfactory by the adult, when it was believed that the situation might develop into an activity of more serious character, or when the mother considered either discontinuance of the activity or delay of progress in the satisfactory solution. *Impedes* differs from *diverts attention* in that no alternative is offered the child. There is no element of danger in the situation.

8. *Forces.*[6] The methods used by the mother to force the child into an activity regardless of his opposition are classified under this heading. The following illustrates the various methods the mother may use: (*a*) force child physically, (*b*) remind child of previous threat, (*c*) use direct commands, or (*d*) call attention to activity of another.

b) Situation: Mother X puts box down in sandpile, then goes to P and says, "Let G play with it awhile. Say 'sorry.' " P cries and mother says, "Stop crying; you remember what I said." J runs over and says, "What is she doing?"

9. *Warns.* *Warns* encompasses those activities of the mother in which there is an element of caution or limitation—sometimes shown in suggestions given the child. For example, the mother may (*a*) suggest a method or methods of avoiding dangers, or (*b*) call attention to danger or limitations.

a) Situation: L pushes K in the wagon. L runs as she pushes the wagon. Mother II goes to L and says, "Be careful not to go too fast; you might strike the jungle gym and hurt K." L looks at mother and goes on pushing K very fast.

10. *Overlooks*[7] (fails to carry through, disregards). In this classification are grouped those methods used by the mother in which she does not, whether intentionally or through carelessness or inadvertence, notice the activities of the child. The mother may (*a*) make a request of the child but carry it out herself before the child complies, (*b*) make a promise and fail to keep it, (*c*) answer her own questions, (*d*) fail to respond to child, or (*e*) give the child an opportunity to choose without abiding by his choice.

e) Situation: Mother VII says, "Do you want to take your suit off, B?" B says, "No." Mother says, "Well, I think you had better have it off. You are too warm." Mother unfastens B's suit and pulls it off.

[6] The term *forces* describes the activities of the mothers used to wear down the child's resistance or opposition so that he is compelled to accept the decision of the mother. The situations classified under *forces* differ from those classified under *urges* and *impedes* in that opposition is shown by the child to the mother, and the mother in turn forces the child into obedience.

[7] *Overlooks* is used here for want of a better term. *Ignores* was discarded because it connotes deliberate and intentional disregard.

11. *Commends.*[8] Under this classification are the methods used
by the mother wherein she expresses her approval, usually through
praise of the child's activities. The mother may (*a*) express approval in terms of the task, (*b*) express approval in terms not related to the task, or (*c*) express approval by physical contact.

b) Situation: G climbs the jungle gym. She puts her right foot
upon the round and holds on with both hands. She stops and looks
around. She climbs upon the second round, holding on with both
hands. She stands up on the round, turns her head, and says, "Look,
Mummy, what I done." Mother II says, "Yes, that's a good girl."

12. *Reassures.*[9] Those activities of the mother which impart to
the child a state of well-being and security in its surroundings be-
long in this category. The mother may (*a*) explain the cause of
the accident or misunderstanding, (*b*) sympathize with the child,
or (*c*) use the presence of another person or herself to reassure
child.

c) Situation: B goes to Mother VII and says, "Where is Miss
T [teacher]?" Mother says, "Miss T went into the house. She
will be back in a few minutes. Go see what the bunny is doing."
B cries and mother says, "Don't cry. She will be back in a few
minutes. Shovel some snow." B says, "No."

13. *Discourages.*[10] The activities of the mother which would
tend to discourage a child from continuing or concluding an activity are grouped under this heading. The mother may (*a*) use an
unfavorable comparison or (*b*) speak disparagingly to the child.

a) Situation: F takes washcloth and stands on basin steps, turns
on water and wets washcloth—then rubs face. Mother VI says,
"You didn't make such a good job, F. C makes a better job than

[8] In situations where the mother's practice is classified as *commends*, her expressions are given *after* the problem is solved, and there is evidence that she
recognizes the results before she commends the child's activities.

[9] *Reassures* describes those activities of the mother which tend to restore the
child's confidence in himself, in adults around him, and in his environment.

[10] The practices included in this classification were found in the situations
where there was evidence that the mother considered the initiation or continua-
tion of an activity unsatisfactory or undesirable. *Discourages* differs from
diverts attention in that no alternative is suggested to the child. The practices
classified under *discourages* differ from those classified under *impedes* in that
they do not have immediate effect upon the progress of the child's activities.

you." F climbs down from basin steps, hangs up washcloth, then dries face on towel.

The observer made a classification, parallel with that of the experimenter, of the mothers' practices upon the basis of the classification outlined on pages 33-38. The experimenter and the observer agreed upon the number of practices included in the group for classification and, when the percentage of agreement with regard to classification was computed, the results showed an agreement of 85 per cent between the experimenter and the observer. Together they studied the practices on whose classification they had disagreed, but no changes were made in the form of classification to be used; for both agreed that further analysis would not improve the classification or add to its objectivity and accuracy.

CLASSIFICATION OF CHILDREN'S ACTIVITIES WITH MOTHERS PARTICIPATING[11]

The following classifications of the children's activities are descriptive of their responses in situations where the mothers were also participants:

1. *Succeeds in carrying out mother's instructions.* The child follows the prescribed course; mother or other children give child no assistance.

2. *Fails to carry out mother's instructions.* Child fails to comply with the instructions of the mother; repeats trials unsuccessfully; requests that assistance be given him by the mother or by other children.

3. *Overlooks instructions.*[12] Child's activities are in opposition to the instructions of the mother; activities are concerned with the solution of another problem.

---

[11] Unless otherwise stated, both mother and child were participants in the activities of the *situations* considered in this section. This section portrays the *children's activities.* The mothers' activities are discussed under "Mothers' Practices."

[12] *Overlooks instructions* entails the description of activities of the child which show his disregard for instructions. These activities cannot, upon the basis of the records, be judged as deliberate and intentional.

4. *Solves problems with assistance.* Child actively participates with another person in the solution of the problem; works co-operatively[13] with mother or with other children.

5. *Does task independently.* Child carries on activities without assistance or guidance from either mother or children.

6. *Requests assistance.* Child verbally requests help.

7. *Expresses inability to do task.* Child verbally admits defeat; repeats unsuccessful attempts to solve problem.

8. *Expresses resistance.* Child fails to obey a verbal request or command by replying with "No," "I won't," or the like; pulls back or refuses to move in response to another person who takes hold of his hand or shoulders; refuses to give up toy or material that another individual asks for or attempts to take; verbally refuses or ignores the methods used by another person to direct, change, or discontinue an activity; uses retaliative measures in defense of himself.

9. *Accepts assistance passively.* Child watches individual who gives assistance; lets things be done for him and to him.

10. *Agrees to suggestion.* Child carries out instruction without hesitation or questioning; verbally expresses approval of suggestion offered.

11. *Expresses insecurity.* Child's expressions show lack of confidence in himself or his environment; expresses uneasiness regarding the activities within the environment; stays very near one person and shows anxiety at the temporary absence of that person from his environment.

12. *Demands property rights.* Child verbally denies the rights of others; holds on to toy or material until decision is given by adult; or until property is rescued from another child or from other children.

13. *Foregoes claim to property.* Child grants permission to use toy or other play material to another child or to other children; withdraws from actively contesting ownership of property.

14. *Attacks child.* Child shows antagonism toward another child

---

[13] *Co-operatively* is employed to describe those activities in which the child works jointly with another child or with the mother for the benefit of both parties involved in the activity.

by hitting, slapping, kicking, or pushing; child's activities show that he is the offender.

15. *Accepts materials.* Child accepts or uses materials or toys offered to him by mother or by other children.

16. *Snatches toy.* Child grabs or takes a toy or any material without the permission of the owner.

17. *Expresses disapproval.* Child fails to co-operate in an activity when solicited by mother or by other children; expresses disapproval, as "I don't want to," "I don't like that," "No."

18. *Expresses an interest.* Child demands information or an explanation; requests to be included as a participant in an activity; watches the development or progress of an activity in which other children are participants.

19. *Requests information.* Child asks questions concerning facts; requests an explanation from mother or children.

20. *Gives information.* Child gives information in reply to a request from mother or other children or in reply to a demand for an explanation.

21. *Expresses a need.* Child points out a need; asks for something.

22. *Offers explanation.* Child attempts, unsolicited by mother or other children, to make clear some object, occurrence, or activity; or to offer another activity in lieu of one that has been requested.

23. *Joins activity.*[14] Child actively participates in activity.

24. *Withdraws.* Child leaves the group in which he has been an active member; ceases from active participation in an activity; pursues another interest or activity.

25. *Calls attention to self or activity.* Child seeks approbation or recognition from the other children or the mother.

26. *Repeats.* Child repeats once or more the words, phrase, or clause that has been used by another child or by the mother.

27. *Cries.* Child's cries may accompany any of the responses described as *resistance*.

28. *Laughs.* Child giggles or makes sounds associated with joy.

[14] *Joins activity* was distinguished from *solves problem with assistance* in that there was no evidence of co-operation or assistance in the former case.

29. *No response.* Child fails to answer a question, a request, or to make a choice.

CLASSIFICATION OF SITUATIONS

The 221 situations were next classified as *routine* and *non-routine* situations upon the basis of similarity found in the problems to be solved by the mothers and those to be solved by the children, or of interests developed in these situations.

A *routine situation* is made up of those activities of mother and child which are involved in the solution of a problem connected with the child's physical comfort and health. These activities were often directed toward establishing acceptable methods for using equipment needed in the physical care of the child and for establishing regularity in the child's habits. The following four situations are classified as *routine*:

1. *Care of wraps and exchange of clothing* includes the activities involved in the exchange of clothing and wraps and the removal of garments from the body, and also those activities of the mother and children involved in the serving of mid-morning lunch, or preparing for the rest period, when clothes and wraps are involved.

2. *Toileting* embraces the activities involved in preparing for and using the toilet and caring for its equipment, and in taking care of the child's hands and clothes following the use of the toilet.

3. *Mid-morning lunch* encompasses the activities involved in preparing, serving, and eating lunch, and in caring for the serving equipment and the hands following the lunch.

4. *Rest* embodies the activities involved in preparing for rest; changing clothes before and after rest; using equipment during rest; and preparing for other activities to be engaged in following the rest period.

A *non-routine situation* includes the activities of the mother and child involved in the use of play equipment and materials; in the individual's development of social techniques acceptable to the group; and in the instruction of the child through play activities or formal and informal instructional periods. The following *non-*

routine situations involve the solution of problems[15] inherent in the activities named above:

1. *Emergency situations* embrace the activities involved in the preservation of the child's comfort or safety, or in helping the child to restore its comfort or safety.

2. *Instructional situations* embody the activities involved in the instruction of the child by the mother through the use of stories, poems, music, games, or modeling in clay.

3. *Free-play situations* embrace the activities involved in the child's direction of the development of his own play interests and progress. *Free play* is further characterized by evidence that the mother entered the situation upon the request of the child after the child had made repeated attempts to solve a problem without success, or after he had showed that he was thwarted in following through an interest or in solving a problem by lack of experience or knowledge in the use of play materials or equipment.

4. *Conflict situations* encompass the activities involved in the settlement of personal and property rights and in disagreements between individual children as evidenced within the group. *Conflict* situations are distinguished from *emergency* situations in that the record shows disputes over personal and property rights and disagreements as to the order or method to be followed in a play activity or the use of play equipment.

The experimenter and the observer again co-operated in segregating and classifying the 221 situations. Each listed the situations independently under the separate headings as defined in the foregoing classification. Upon comparing the results of the two separate tallies, and upon computing the percentage of agreement, an agreement of 87 per cent between the experimenter and her as-

---

[15] The distinction the experimenter makes between *situations* and *problems* arising within the situations is based upon the definition of *situation*; that is, the activities of mother and child as grouped around the solution of problems or the development of an interest. For example, in the *toileting situation*, the mother may recognize a *problem* which causes her to warn the child of danger, but this problem is incidental to the success involved in preparing for and using the toilet and in making preparation for other activities in which the child is interested.

sistant was found in the classification of the situations analyzed in the Nursery School records of this study.

CLASSIFICATION OF CERTAIN BEHAVIOR TRENDS AS DETERMINED BY CONTACTS MADE BY THE CHILDREN[16]

In order to study the behavior of individual children in the Nursery School, another classification was made. The children's activities were classified according to contacts. A *contact*, as defined in this study, is the verbal or physical exchange between one child and another child or other children. A contact was considered as *initiated* when the verbal or physical stimulus of the one child was recognized and responded to by the other child or children. The contact was considered *finished* when the first child failed to respond to stimuli verbally or physically expressed by another child or by other children, or when one of the participants withdrew from the group and began to develop a new activity.

The records used for this part of the study were those of one child's activities in relation to another child or to other children. Some of the contacts studied were taken from the mothers' records, but no distinct analysis was made of the children's activities in which the mother was a participant.

Any relationship between the practices of the mother and the behavior trends of the child evidenced in this study is merely a suggestive one. The data used herein are inadequate for determining any conclusive relationship between the mother's behavior and the child's responses.

The following six forms of behavior were selected as indicative of the behavior trends revealed through the children's contacts:

1. *Co-operative* behavior describes the contacts of the children when their activities show that the participants assume joint responsibility in the development of a play interest or in the solution of a problem; or share, voluntarily or upon request, play equipment or play materials.

[16] No attempt was made by the experimenter to study *all* the behavior trends in evidence in the contacts made by the children in the Nursery School.

2. Under *initiative* behavior are classified those activities of the child which show independence in developing a group activity, leadership in the solution of a problem in a group contact, the use of pertinent and acceptable suggestions in the improvement of group play, and the development of a play activity from a group interest.

3. *Aggressiveness*[17] embodies such activities as dictating the activity of the group (self-assertiveness), demanding attention from the group by giving commands, grabbing or taking without owner's consent toys or play materials, and the child's demanding that his wishes be accepted by another child or by other children.

4. *Resistance* embraces those contacts in which the child, by his activities, shows unwillingness to obey a verbal request or command as evidenced by withdrawal when approached by another child; by refusal to discontinue an activity when interrupted or opposed by another person or when any change is suggested in an activity; by crying or by some other form of opposition to verbal or physical stimulus, such as saying, "Don't," "No," "I won't."

5. *Combative* behavior[18] denotes the type of contact the child makes when he engages in conflicts or makes an attack, either as defender or aggressor, upon another child by slapping, kicking, knocking, or striking with something.

6. *Resourcefulness* refers to those contacts in which the child shows independence in the management of equipment in routine situations, or unusual ability to use play material or play equipment to express his interests or experiences.

Five hundred fifty contacts were listed by the observer and the experimenter, each making an independent classification. Upon totaling the number of agreements and computing the percentage, the results showed an agreement of 95 per cent in the use of the classification designed for grouping the behavior exhibited by the children in their contacts.

[17] The positive activities of this type of behavior are classed under *initiative* behavior.

[18] *Combative* behavior is recognized as one method of showing resistance. It was studied separately to discover the frequency with which these children resorted to this type of resistance.

SUMMARY

1. An examination of the eleven mothers' records showed that their activities and those of the fourteen children centered, in each case, around common problems or interests. These related activities the experimenter termed *situations*.

2. An analysis of the situations showed similarities in their competent activities, both for mothers and for children. Using these similarities as a basis, the experimenter classified the activities of the mothers, designated as *practices*, under thirteen main headings; for example, *directs, seeks information, offers explanation, diverts attention*.

3. These practices were in turn analyzed in terms of *methods* used by the mothers in carrying out their practices. Example: Mother may *direct* by (*a*) telling the child that the equipment belongs to him, (*b*) telling the child to place the toy, equipment, or clothing in a certain place or in a certain way, or giving the child the order of routine, (*c*) telling the child to co-operate or to share in the use of equipment, etc.

4. The activities of the children recorded in the situations in which the mothers were participants were classified under twenty-nine headings on the basis of similarity of response.

5. The situations were further studied and divided, upon the basis of problems to be solved or interests to be developed, into *routine* and *non-routine situations, respectively*. The four *routine* situations were *care of wraps and exchange of clothing, toileting, mid-morning lunch,* and *rest*; the four *non-routine* situations, *emergency, instructional, free play,* and *conflict*.

6. A study of the records of the activities of the children in relation to one another indicated that the children's behavior might be classified as follows: *co-operative, aggressive, resistant, combative, resourceful,* and *initiatory*.

7. The experimenter and the observer were found to be in agreement in 85, 87, and 95 per cent of the cases in their respective classifications of the mothers' practices, the classification of situations, and the classification of children's behavior as exhibited in their contacts with other children.

Chapter IV

ANALYSIS OF MOTHERS' PRACTICES AND CHILDREN'S ACTIVITIES IN THE NURSERY SCHOOL SITUATION

IN THIS chapter an analysis is made of (1) the type and number of practices used by the mothers in the routine and non-routine situations, (2) the practices directed toward the individual child, and (3) the activities of the children during the period each mother was observed.[1] Additional data were furnished by the opportunities which the experimenter had to make contacts with the mothers and with the children in their homes, and also through longer periods of observation in the Nursery School than those afforded the observer in making records. The additional data were used by the experimenter to supplement the interpretation of the data presented in tables.

NUMBER AND DISTRIBUTION OF THE THIRTEEN PRACTICES USED BY THE ELEVEN MOTHERS

The eleven mothers used 3,716 practices during the nine hours of observation allotted to each mother in directing the fourteen children in routine and non-routine situations. Table I shows the number and distribution of the 3,716 practices as recorded for each of the eleven mothers. The mothers varied in their use of the practices from the 477 shown in Mother I's record to the 211 recorded at the time Mother II was observed. Mother VIII ranked second in the number of practices used, her record showing 457 practices; Mother VI ranked third, her record containing 374 practices; Mother IX used 350 practices; Mother X's record of 344 practices was closely paralleled by Mother XI's record of 339 practices, and ranked fourth, while Mothers III and VII ranked

---

[1] See Chapters II and III for definitions of *practice, situation,* and *activity* as used in the present chapter.

TABLE

NUMBER AND DISTRIBUTION OF THE 3,716 PRACTICES

PRAC

Mother	Total No. of Practices	Seeks Information		Offers Explanation		Diverts Attention		Urges		Directs		Encourages	
		No.	Per Cent	No.	Per Cent	No.	Per Cent	No.	Per Cent	No.	Per Cent	No.	Per Cent
I ..	477	52	10.9	54	11.3	19	3.9	10	2.3	254	53.2	16	3.3
II ..	211	24	11.4	24	11.4	4	1.8	7	3.5	111	52.6	18	8.7
III ..	315	20	6.4	32	10.1	15	4.8	2	0.6	182	57.7	12	3.8
IV ..	266	24	9.0	21	7.8	3	1.1	5	1.8	153	57.8	17	6.5
V ..	268	30	11.1	35	12.9	4	1.5	2	0.7	106	39.8	25	9.3
VI ..	374	51	13.3	65	17.3	14	3.4	13	3.2	161	43.0	16	4.2
VII ..	315	32	10.2	27	8.6	8	2.5	18	5.7	180	57.1	9	2.9
VIII ..	457	36	7.7	29	6.3	4	0.9	7	1.5	280	61.2	22	4.8
IX ..	350	38	10.8	24	6.8	13	3.8	24	6.8	170	48.7	24	6.8
X ..	344	40	11.7	29	8.4	10	2.9	3	0.9	178	51.8	23	6.6
XI ..	339	42	12.4	46	13.8	11	3.5	11	3.5	147	44.4	23	6.8
Total	3,716	389	10.5	386	10.4	105	2.8	102	2.7	1,922	51.7	205	5.5

fifth, as each used 315 practices; and Mothers V and IV occupied the sixth place and were next to Mother II, who used the fewest practices, as they each used 268 and 266 practices when they served as assistants in the Nursery School.

The thirteen practices are discussed below in the order of the frequency of their use. Twelve of the practices are discussed in pairs, since each of the paired practices closely paralleled the other in frequency of use. *Directs* is the only practice that is considered by itself.

Directs. This practice was used more frequently than any other practice by the mothers as a group, and also by the mothers individually. As shown in Table I, *directs* constitutes 51.7 per cent of the total number of mothers' practices. The frequency of the use of *directs* by individual mothers varies from 61.2 per cent in the case of Mother VIII to 39.8 per cent in the case of Mother V. Six of the mothers, including Mothers, I, II, III, IV, VII, and X, show records in which more than 50 per cent of their practices are classified as *directs*, and the remaining three records of Mothers

I

USED BY THE MOTHERS IN THE NURSERY SCHOOL

TICES

Impedes		Forces		Warns		Overlooks		Commends		Reassures		Discourages	
No.	Per Cent	No.	Per Cent	No.	Per Cent	No.	Per Cent	No.	Per Cent	No.	Per Cent	No.	Per Cent
18	3.7	2	0.5	1	0.2	34	7.8	13	2.7	3	0.6	1	0.2
7	3.3	..	...	2	0.9	7	3.3	2	0.9	4	1.8	1	0.4
21	6.6	2	0.6	3	1.0	8	2.5	8	2.5	7	2.2	3	0.9
10	3.7	..	...	2	0.7	6	2.2	19	7.2	6	2.2	..	...
44	16.6	..	...	3	1.1	7	2.6	7	2.6	3	1.1	2	0.7
14	3.7	2	0.7	3	0.9	14	3.7	12	3.5	4	1.5	5	1.6
19	6.0	1	0.3	7	2.2	10	3.1	1	0.3	3	0.9	..	...
24	5.5	1	0.2	6	1.3	11	2.4	36	7.7	1	0.2	..	...
13	3.7	..	...	7	2.0	10	2.8	16	4.5	9	2.8	2	0.5
22	6.4	3	0.9	4	1.1	8	2.4	8	2.4	16	4.6	..	...
16	4.8	6	1.8	3	0.8	17	5.1	4	1.2	7	2.1	6	1.8
208	5.6	17	0.5	41	1.1	132	3.6	126	3.4	63	1.7	20	0.5

VI, IX, and XI show 43.0 per cent, 48.7 per cent, and 44.4 per cent of their practices classified in the same category.

Seeks Information and *Offers Explanation*. An analysis of the practices used by the eleven mothers shows 10.5 per cent of the total number classified as *seeks information* and 10.4 per cent as *offers explanation*. These two classes of practices rank second in frequency to *directs* and were used with almost the same frequency by the mothers as a group and as individuals. The records of the mothers' practices show that Mother VI used *seeks information* the most frequently of any member of the group, with 13.3 per cent of her practices classified under this heading. Mother III used this type of practice least frequently, her records showing 6.4 per cent of her practices grouped in this category. Mother VI ranks first in the use of the *offers explanation* practices, her records showing 17.3 per cent of her practices listed in this category. Mother VIII ranks last in her use of the practices classified as *offers explanation*, with 6.3 per cent of her practices grouped in this category.

Encourages and *Impedes*. *Encourages* shows a parallel frequency with *impedes* for the group as a whole, with 5.5 per cent of the practices used by the group classified as *encourages* and 5.6 per cent as *impedes*. The data show a variation in the use of *encourages* from 9.3 per cent of the total practices in the records of Mother V to 2.9 per cent of the total in the records of Mother VII. The frequency of the use of *impedes* varies from 16.6 per cent of the total number of Mother V's practices to the low record of 3.3 per cent of the total number of Mother II's practices.

Commends and *Overlooks*. Each set of practices classified as *commends* and *overlooks* ranks third in frequency of use by the eleven mothers as a group. The mothers' records show 3.4 per cent of their practices classified as *commends* and 3.6 per cent as *overlooks*. The records of the individuals show the frequency of use of *commends* varying from 7.7 per cent observed in Mother VIII's record to 0.3 per cent in Mother VII's record; and of *overlooks*, from 7.8 per cent in the case of Mother I to 2.2 per cent in that of Mother IV.

Diverts Attention and *Urges*. In frequency of use, 2.8 per cent of the practices of the mothers are classified as *diverts attention*, and this percentage is closely paralleled by that for *urges*. In the class, *urges*, 2.7 per cent of the total number of practices are found. Mother III used *diverts attention* more frequently than any other mother in the group, showing a frequency of 4.8 per cent of her total number of practices thus classified, whereas Mother VIII had the lowest record for the group. Of her total number of practices, *diverts attention* has a frequency of 0.9 per cent. The individual frequency in the use of *urges* varies from 6.8 per cent of the total number of practices in the case of Mother IX to 0.6 per cent in the case of Mother III.

Reassures and *Warns*. *Reassures* and *warns* show a comparable distribution in the total number of practices recorded for the group, 1.7 per cent of the practices being classified as *reassures* and 1.1 per cent as *warns*. *Reassures* varies in individual frequency from 4.6 per cent in Mother X's record to 0.2 per cent in Mother VIII's record. *Warns* varies in use from 2.2 per cent in the case of Mother VII to 0.7 per cent in the case of Mother IV.

Discourages and *Forces*. The occurrence of practices classified under the categories of *discourages* and *forces* is in each case only 0.5 per cent of the total number of practices. However, these practices show variation in use when the records of the individual mothers are compared.[2] *Discourages* was employed with the greatest frequency by Mother XI and with the least frequency by Mother I, accounting for 1.8 per cent and 0.2 per cent, respectively, of the total number of their practices. In the case of *forces*, variations in individual frequency range from Mother XI's relatively high record of 1.8 per cent to Mother VIII's relatively low record of 0.2 per cent. *Discourages* and *forces* are the only practices not found in the records of every mother. Mothers IV, VII, VIII, and X were not observed using the practice classified as *discourages*; and the records of Mothers II, IV, V, and IX show the absence of the practice designated as *forces*.

RELATIVE FREQUENCY OF PRACTICES USED BY
MOTHERS IN ROUTINE AND NON-ROUTINE
SITUATIONS

Table II gives the total number of situations and the total number of practices used in each of the routine and non-routine situations by the group and by the individual mothers. Detailed analyses were made of the variety of practices of the individual mothers for each of the eight routine and non-routine situations. The significant data have been simplified and included in Table II.

The eleven mothers, during the observation periods, participated in 602 routine and non-routine situations, as shown in Table II. Of this number, 30.1 per cent of the situations participated in by the mothers were observed in the solution of *toileting* problems; 14.6 per cent in the *care of wraps and exchange of clothing*; 14.1 per cent in situations in which children were participants in *free play*. Eleven and eight-tenths per cent of the situations participated in by the mothers were observed in the *instructional* periods; 10.7

---

[2] A number of tables were drawn up to note general trends but are not reproduced in this volume. However, such trends as were revealed have been utilized in the more special interpretations of data.

TABLE II

NUMBER AND PER CENT OF PRACTICES USED IN EACH ROUTINE AND NON-ROUTINE SITUATION

Mother	Total No. of Situations	Total No. of Practices Used	Routine Situation								Non-Routine Situation							
			Clothing		Toilet		Lunch		Rest		Emergency		Instruction		Free Play		Conflicts	
			No.	Per Cent	No.	Per Cent	No.	Per Cent	No.	Per Cent	No.	Per Cent	No.	Per Cent	No.	Per Cent	No.	Per Cent
I	52	477	51	10.7	145	30.4	19	3.9	87	18.2	35	7.3	104	22.0	36	7.5	..	..
II	44	211	19	9.0	69	32.7	19	9.0	11	5.2	21	10.0	52	24.6	14	6.6	6	2.8
III	64	315	52	16.5	100	31.2	24	7.6	..	..	26	8.3	67	21.3	24	7.6	22	7.0
IV	65	266	58	21.8	95	35.7	29	10.9	9	3.4	18	6.8	18	6.8	28	10.5	11	4.5
V	37	268	23	8.6	96	35.8	16	6.0	..	..	2	0.7	44	16.4	61	22.8	26	9.7
VI	83	374	61	16.3	68	18.1	30	8.0	49	13.1	30	8.0	68	18.1	59	15.8	9	2.4
VII	44	315	70	22.2	117	37.1	34	10.0	56	17.8	10	3.2	2	0.6	19	6.0	7	2.2
VIII	48	457	40	8.7	295	64.5	53	11.5	24	5.3	17	3.7	5	1.1	23	5.0	..	..
IX	63	350	61	17.4	34	9.7	20	5.7	102	29.1	33	9.4	18	5.1	77	22.0	5	1.4
X	63	344	52	15.1	83	24.1	37	10.8	5	0.1	20	5.8	24	7.0	98	28.5	25	7.3
XI	39	339	53	9.0	33	9.7	39	11.5	56	16.5	22	6.5	39	11.5	82	24.2	15	4.4
Total	602	3,716	540	14.6	1,135	30.1	320	8.7	399	10.7	234	6.3	441	11.8	521	14.1	126	3.5

per cent in the solution of *rest* problems; 8.7 per cent in *mid-morning lunch* situations, which fact may be partially explained by the size and kind of equipment used in service of the lunch. The records showed that 6.3 per cent of the situations were observed at the time the mothers and children were solving problems of *emergency*, and 3.5 per cent in situations in which children were engaged in *conflicts*.

The number of situations participated in by the individuals varied: Mothers IV and III ranked first, with recorded participation in 65 and 64 situations, respectively; Mothers IX and X each entered into 63 situations; Mother I's record shows that she entered into 52 situations; and the records of practices for Mothers VIII, II, VII, XI, and V are tabulated in 48, 44, 44, 39, and 37 situations, respectively.

When the records of the eleven mothers were examined and a comparative study was made of the four routine situations and the four non-routine situations, differences were shown (1) in the frequency with which the mothers participated in the various situations, and (2) in the number and types of practices used by the eleven mothers as a group and as individuals in assisting the children in the eight routine and non-routine situations. The data tabulated in Table II were used as the basis for these comparisons.

In the 602 routine and non-routine situations in which the mothers participated, as shown in Table II, the eleven mothers used 3,716 practices. The largest number of practices was used by the mothers in guiding the children in the *toileting* situation, with 30.1 per cent of the practices relating to this situation. The group of situations in which the mothers used the next largest number of practices was the *care of wraps and exchange of clothing* and *free play* situations, requiring 14.6 per cent and 14.1 per cent, respectively, of the total number of practices. Of the total number of practices employed by the mothers, 11.8 per cent related to *instructional* situations, 10.7 per cent to *rest* situations, 8.7 per cent to *mid-morning lunch* situations, and 3.5 per cent, the fewest practices, to situations in which the children were involved in *conflicts*.

Differences were shown in the various situations in the type and frequency with which the eleven mothers used the different practices in guiding the children. The mothers' records show that the members of the group chose to use the practices listed in each of the thirteen classes in assisting the children in the *toileting* situations, during *free play*, and when they were active in the *instructional* situations. The following seven practices were chosen by members of the group in each of the routine and non-routine situations : *seeks information, offers explanation, urges, directs, encourages, impedes,* and *overlooks.* The practice, *diverts attention,* was used in seven of the eight situations. This practice was omitted by the group from the *mid-morning lunch* situations. The practices classified as *forces* were used in only one routine situation, *toileting,* and in the four non-routine situations, including *emergencies, instruction, free play,* and *conflicts.* The practice, *warns,* was omitted from the *rest* situations and included in the other three routine situations, omitted from the *conflict* situations, and chosen for the remaining three non-routine situations. The mothers chose to *commend* the children in all instances except *emergency* situations. Methods of *reassurance* were used in the three routine situations, including *care of wraps and exchange of clothing, toileting,* and *rest* periods, and omitted from the *mid-morning lunch* situations; likewise, *reassurance* techniques were evident in the non-routine situations, including *free play, instruction,* and *emergency,* and omitted from *conflicts.* The practice described as *discourages* was used in the smallest number of situations of any of the practices. This group of mothers chose this practice as they assisted the children in *toileting, rest, free play,* and *instructional* situations, and failed to use it in *care of wraps and exchange of clothing, mid-morning lunch, emergency,* and *conflict* situations.

The records of the practices used in the routine and non-routine situations show that members of the group chose a wider range of practices in the *toileting, free play,* and *instructional* situations than in any other of the eight situations, as practices were included from each of the thirteen classes. The mothers chose fewer types of practices as they assisted the children in the *care of wraps and exchange of clothing* situations, in the *rest* periods, and in the two non-routine situations, *emergencies* and *conflicts;* eleven of the thirteen practices were chosen in the first three situations named, and ten practices were used in solving problems when the children were involved in *conflicts*. In the *mid-morning lunch* situations, the practices were restricted to nine types, the narrowest range of choice. The practices used most frequently in *mid-morning lunch* situations included *directs, seeks information, offers explanation, impedes, urges, commends, encourages, warns,* and *overlooks,* listed in the order of frequency used in directing the children.

Some of the conditions under which the mothers assisted the children in the Nursery School seemed to influence the mothers in the frequency with which they participated and the practices they chose in some of the routine situations. At the *mid-morning lunch* the mothers served orange juice, tomato juice, or milk, if the request came from home. Large pitchers and trays were used for the serving, and this equipment proved too heavy for the children to manipulate. Further on in this study it is revealed that the practices used in the *lunch* situation were restricted to nine types, which number showed the narrowest range in choice of practices observed in the routine and non-routine situations. It is probable that a greater variety of practices, as well as a different distribution of use, would have been observed if such changes as the following had been initiated in the usual situation:

1. If a regular meal had been served at lunch (with the possibility of a poor appetite in some cases), if a greater variety of foods had been included (in view of the possibility of certain children disliking certain foods), or if different equipment had been used which allowed more participation by the children in the service of the lunch.

2. If the equipment in the bathrooms had been suitable for children instead of adults. Temporary improvisations were necessary, and the children were unable to use the toileting equipment efficiently and with ease.

3. If the clothing, both indoor and outdoor, provided for the children had allowed for more manipulation by the children. Frequently the mothers' assistance was required in making minor adjustments, and the children were unable to change their outside garments without adult help.

In each of the routine situations the mothers demonstrated an interest in the development of effective habits in one or more of the following situations: *toileting, rest,* and *care of clothing.* This interest seemed to influence the number of times they entered the given situation and guided the children in solving problems of corresponding type. There were mothers in the group who gave special attention to one or more of the problems in routine situations and who apparently allowed the difficulties they were experiencing with their own child in such situations to influence them in their methods of handling the problems which arose.

When a comparison was made of the number and type of practices observed in the various situations and the frequency with which the mothers participated, apparently the following factors were the ones that motivated the mothers: first, their appraisal of the problems and the behavior they observed in the situation; second, their attitude toward their own responsibility in providing leadership for the children of this age; and third, their individual interests in certain activities.

The experimenter learned from observation that the mothers appraised the factors and elements in each situation in which they were concerned. Apparently, the individual's appraisal of the problems largely determined her guidance. One group of mothers, Mothers I, III, V, VIII, and XI, employed guidance methods that indicated a careful survey of the problems encountered by the children. Each displayed some knowledge of the children's ability to take care of themselves in the use of equipment and in the adjustment of personal and group difficulties. Apparently these mothers observed the difficulties and calmly directed the children when they judged the children's experience and technique to be inadequate, or entered into the situation at the appeal of one of the children or to protect a child from injury or further insult. On the other hand, Mother II seemed to feel an unusual responsibility for the safety of the children. Seemingly, this one factor influenced her in judging the difficulties the children were experiencing and in restricting the children's play activities to the use of familiar equipment, and in the close supervision which she gave the child who was experimenting with personal and group relationships.

Mother II appeared to study the situations to detect any activity for which she could *commend* and *encourage* the child and for which she might *reassure* the child. Her records revealed infrequent use of the practice, *warns,* and practices which apparently were chosen for the purpose of distracting the child's attention and changing his activities. Mother II's behavior revealed two characteristics which seemed to influence her decisions to enter into the child's activity. These two characteristics were the restrictions she imposed upon the children's activities because of her fear of experimentation and exploration on the part of the children and her prejudices against certain behavior, such as disagreements and arguments, which expressed the child's dissatisfaction in a situation.

Mothers V and X each exhibited an intolerant attitude toward certain behavior expressed by their children, D and P. When either D or P displayed any dependence upon their mothers, the practices of Mothers V and X revealed their impatience with the child. These mothers seemed to be more tolerant when the same behavior was displayed by children other than their own in comparatively the same situations in which they had shown intolerance.

Another factor, described as the influence of the mothers' feeling of responsibility in providing leadership in the group, seemed to influence Mother VI in her participation in the group more than any other mother. She frequently entered into each of the situations and directed the children's attention, through the practices she selected, to adult interests, apparently ignoring those shown by the children. She seemed to be unaware of the children's attempts at leadership and insisted upon "something happening." Other mothers, including Mothers III, V, and XI, appeared to be concerned over the direction of the younger children's interests and frequently directed the attention of B, C, D, F, H, P, and Q to feasible interests. However, these three mothers exhibited more understanding of the children's attempts and withdrew as soon as a child began the exploration of any interest. Mothers IV, II, and IX were observed participating relatively frequently in different situations; however, they showed a decided interest in their own children's problems. Their children, C, G, H, and I, each exhibited dependence in the initiation and in the following through of individual interests.

In many instances the mothers apparently entered into and directed the children's activities toward the non-routine situations because the activity represented their individual interests. Mother I frequently displayed much interest in the children's experience with clay and many times modeled with the children, often demonstrating various forms as she handled the clay. Mother II's behavior revealed she was interested in teaching, as her records contained many instances in both routine and non-routine situations in which she *offered explanations*, by pointing out facts, and questioned the children, using a teacher's formal methods of instruction. Likewise, Mothers I, III, V, VI, IX, X, and XI all were interested in teaching, although these mothers displayed more respect for the child's interests than did Mother II in that they limited their teaching to the *instructional* periods. Mother X exhibited interest in music, and frequently directed the children's interest and attention to problems of rhythm. She insisted that her own child, P, participate in all activities in which music was used.

In addition, two other factors were observed which apparently influenced the mothers more consistently in their choice of practices than those described above. One of these factors previously described was the desire for and the use of efficient methods of directing children in the solution of problems. These parents displayed interest in accomplishing quickly recognizable results. This interest apparently influenced them in the frequent choice of *directs* as a practice, and seemed to outweigh the one in which the guidance techniques were selected because the method furnished valuable training to the individual child. Another factor was the mothers' attempts to establish rapport with the children by the use of certain practices frequently observed when the mother was alone with a child and when she was alone with a small group of children. In these more intimate situations, questions were asked which seemed not to demand an answer, explanations were elaborately given, and the mother's directions were expressed along with irrelevant statements.

NUMBER AND TYPES OF PRACTICES USED BY
MOTHERS IN DIRECTING EACH CHILD

Table III reveals the total number of practices used by the eleven mothers in directing the children in the Nursery School, and the number of times the mothers used the practices in directing the individuals. C was directed most frequently. Her record shows 546 practices used by the mothers in assisting her in the Nursery School during the nine hours of observation time assigned to her; during the same period of time, 172 practices were directed toward A as he participated in the Nursery School. The second group of children who were directed relatively frequently and whose records show comparable frequencies included F, with 480 practices; D, with 470 practices; and B, with 439 practices. The third group classed together on the basis of frequency included G, with 380 practices; P, with 353 practices; and Q, with 320 practices. The fourth group included the largest number 'of children, as follows: H, 287 practices; J, 246 practices; I, 245 practices; K, 221 practices; E, 221 practices; and L, 207 practices. C and A were classed alone in the highest and lowest groups, respectively.

A study of the frequency with which each child was directed by the different practices revealed similarities in the frequency with which the mothers used the five practices, including *directs, encourages, impedes, seeks information,* and *offers explanation* in guiding each child in the group. The children were most frequently instructed in the procedures which they were to follow by *directs*.

An examination revealed that certain practices appeared with comparable frequency in the records of the eleven children and in the records of individual children. For example, when the records were compared, *seeks information* and *offers explanation* showed the similarity just referred to, and the same was true in the use of *encourages* and *impedes*.

A similarity was noted in the records of individual children of the infrequent use of the practices, *forces, reassures,* and *discourages*.

In reviewing the records of individual children, the experi-

TABLE

TYPES OF PRACTICES USED BY

PRAC

Child	Total No. of Practices	Seeks Information		Offers Explanation		Diverts Attention		Urges		Directs		Encourages	
		No.	Per Cent	No.	Per Cent	No.	Per Cent	No.	Per Cent	No.	Per Cent	No.	Per Cent
A	172	37	21.5	24	14.0	7	4.1	4	2.2	58	33.7	17	9.9
B	439	48	10.9	23	5.3	23	5.2	14	3.2	228	51.9	26	5.9
C	546	73	13.4	39	7.2	10	1.8	11	2.0	265	48.5	38	7.0
D	470	26	5.5	35	7.4	16	3.4	23	4.9	260	55.3	28	5.9
E	221	24	10.9	36	16.3	17	7.7	4	1.8	87	39.4	13	5.8
F	480	68	14.1	42	8.8	13	2.7	15	3.2	223	46.4	29	6.1
G	380	64	16.9	33	8.7	4	1.0	8	2.1	190	50.0	32	8.4
H	287	43	15.0	20	7.0	6	2.1	11	3.8	150	52.3	19	6.6
I	245	41	16.7	30	12.3	8	3.4	..	...	123	50.1	13	5.1
J	246	21	8.5	45	18.3	20	8.1	4	1.6	93	37.8	10	4.1
K	221	29	13.1	45	20.4	13	5.9	4	1.8	87	39.4	10	4.5
L	207	24	11.6	31	15.0	3	1.4	2	0.9	105	50.7	13	6.4
P	353	9	2.8	32	9.1	10	2.8	4	1.3	213	60.0	28	7.9
Q	320	12	3.8	27	8.4	10	3.1	4	1.3	198	61.8	23	7.2
Total	4,587	519	11.4	462	10.1	160	3.4	108	2.3	2,280	49.8	299	6.5

menter found that there were individuals in the group whose characteristics as revealed in the group encouraged the mothers in the use of the same practices, while other children's behavior apparently caused the mothers to be more selective in practices based upon the personal characteristics of the child. The experimenter recognizes insufficient data to establish this relationship; however, these characteristics seemed to have some influence upon the mother's selection of practices.

The independence of the child apparently was one factor which prejudiced the mothers in favor of certain practices in guiding the individual child. This factor was revealed by comparing the practices directed toward one group of children, A, E, J, K, and L, who were independent in the development of their interests and in routine activities, with the ones selected for guiding the more dependent and younger children. J, E, and K were independent in

III

MOTHERS IN DIRECTING EACH CHILD

TICES

Impedes		Forces		Warns		Overlooks		Commends		Reassures		Discourages	
No.	Per Cent	No.	Per Cent	No.	Per Cent	No.	Per Cent	No.	Per Cent	No.	Per Cent	No.	Per Cent
4	2.2	..	...	7	4.1	1	0.6	9	5.4	3	1.7	1	0.6
28	6.4	2	0.4	2	0.4	14	3.2	20	4.6	11	2.5	..	...
29	5.4	1	0.1	6	1.1	33	6.0	33	6.0	7	1.3	1	0.1
25	5.4	2	0.4	6	1.6	27	5.7	20	4.0	..	...	2	0.4
14	6.3	1	0.5	6	2.7	6	2.7	9	4.1	4	1.8	..	...
27	5.6	2	0.4	12	2.5	17	3.5	31	6.5	..	...	1	0.2
7	1.8	..	...	..	...	21	5.5	10	2.6	11	2.9	..	...
8	2.8	..	...	2	0.7	19	6.6	3	1.0	6	2.1	..	...
12	4.9	..	...	4	1.6	1	0.4	5	2.0	6	2.4	2	0.8
17	6.9	2	0.8	11	4.6	15	6.1	1	0.4	1	0.4	6	2.4
11	5.0	1	0.4	7	3.2	4	1.8	4	1.8	2	0.9	4	1.8
16	7.7	..	...	2	0.9	9	4.3	..	...	1	0.4	1	0.4
18	5.1	6	1.7	7	2.0	7	2.0	4	1.1	10	2.8	5	1.4
16	5.0	2	0.6	6	1.9	1	0.3	12	3.8	9	2.8	..	...
232	5.1	19	0.3	78	1.3	175	3.8	161	3.6	71	1.6	23	0.5

their initiation of activities and in their explorations and experimentations in the Nursery School. L was dominated by K and carried out his dictations, a fact which gave her a place in the group. A fitted into the group by assuming responsibilities that were minor and aided J, E, or K in the development of their interests. The children J, E, K, and L were guided by such practices as *seeks information, urges, encourages, impedes, reassures,* and *offers explanation* more frequently than any other members of the group. L, who was the least independent member, was frequently aided in her activities by *directs*. A, who was slower in his movements and less imaginative in his interests than the other members of the group, was *encouraged* and never *forced* into any activity. The other group, made up of the less mature and less independent children, G, C, F, H, I, and Q, was more frequently guided by *directs, seeks information, offers explanation, warns,* and *overlooks*.

Other characteristics revealed by G, B, C, F, and Q led the experimenter to surmise from her contacts in the group that behavior of these individuals was partially responsible for the guidance directed toward them. G lacked self-confidence and frequently exhibited fear; she was never guided by the method classified as *warns*. The mothers were observed guiding her with such practices as *encouragement, commendation,* and *reassurance.* B, who rarely exhibited fear, displayed ability beyond his chronological age in handling play equipment. Frequent use of *diverts attention* indicated that certain mothers lacked confidence in B's skill to manipulate the comparatively advanced play equipment. C, who found the adjustment to the Nursery School a long and tedious task, frequently resorted to asking the mothers many questions to which they as a rule responded by giving explicit explanations. She feigned distress and difficulty in the use of equipment and in cooperative projects with other children, to secure the mothers' attention, which they gave by carefully directing her, using methods of *encouragement* and many times of *commendation.* By observing C's behavior over a period of time, the experimenter concluded that C was ingenious in getting the mothers to perform for her benefit. F, who was given very little freedom at home and only limited opportunities to initiate and to follow through his interests, was given much freedom by the mothers as they guided him. Methods were used to give him assurance, and seldom was he thwarted in his efforts by the mothers' leadership. Q, whose home conditions were such that she found difficulty in gaining a feeling of security in the Nursery School, was in many instances guided by practices described as *reassurance* and *commendation.* Her records failed to show the use of *discouragement.*

PRACTICES USED BY THE ELEVEN MOTHERS IN DIRECTING OWN CHILD AND OTHER CHILDREN

Table III shows the total number of practices used by the eleven mothers in directing each of the children. The experimenter tabulated the practices directed by the mother toward her own child and those practices used by the mothers in directing other children. A summary of this tabulated information is presented in Table IV, showing that a total of 1,878 practices[3] was used by the mothers in directing their own children, and 2,270 practices in directing other children. The percentage of the practices used in directing the mother's own child was tabulated for each of the eleven mothers, and the total percentage of each practice used by the mothers was divided by eleven in order to show the practices chosen by the "average mother" as she directed her own child. The same procedure was followed in determining the practices used by the mothers in directing other children. The results of this tabulation, as graphically presented in Chart I, show that the "average" mother preferred *overlooks, seeks information, offers explanation, encourages, commends,* and *warns,* in directing her own child. As they directed children belonging to other mothers, the members of this group showed a preference for *reassures, diverts attention, impedes, directs, urges, forces,* and *discourages.*

A comparison was made of the frequency with which the mothers directed their own children and the frequency with which they directed children belonging to other mothers. The total number and the distribution of practices used by the "average" mother in directing the "average" own child and the "average" other child were based upon the results obtained in the previous calculations in determining the percentage of practices used by the "average" mother. The number of practices chosen by the "average" mother was divided by thirteen to determine the practices and the frequency with which the "average" mother directed the "average" own child and the "average" other child. The results of these tabulations are presented in Table IV and graphically shown in Chart I.

The results of the comparison of the practices selected by the mothers in directing their own children as against other children suggested the presence of an "emotional factor" described as *sympathetic* and *protective.* The mothers' practices indicated an understanding of the child and of his or her problems which may

[3] The total number of practices tabulated in Table III does not equal the number shown in Table IV, as Child B's record was not included in the latter tabulation. B's mother did not serve as assistant in the Nursery School.

TABLE IV

MOTHERS' PRACTICES DIRECTED TOWARD "AVERAGE" OWN CHILD AND
"AVERAGE" OTHER CHILDREN

Mothers' Practices	Total Number of Practices		Practices Directed to "Average" Own Child		Practices Directed to "Average" Other Children	
	Toward Own Child	Toward Other Children	Average Per Cent	Average Number	Average Per Cent	Average Number
Directs	780	1,278	47.0	52.3	56.2	90.1
Seeks information.......	261	210	12.6	20.7	8.2	16.1
Offers explanation.......	286	153	13.6	22.0	7.2	11.7
Impedes......	96	108	5.4	7.4	5.8	8.1
Encourages ..	151	122	6.2	11.6	4.8	9.4
Overlooks ...	85	76	3.8	6.5	3.4	5.9
Commends ..	75	66	3.6	5.9	3.2	5.0
Diverts attention	55	82	2.4	4.6	3.4	6.3
Urges	33	66	2.2	4.4	3.2	5.0
Warns	29	20	1.5	2.5	0.7	1.5
Reassures ...	20	56	1.0	1.6	2.7	4.3
Discourages ..	4	19	0.3	0.3	0.7	1.3
Forces	3	14	0.3	0.2	0.7	1.0
Total	1,878	2,270	100.0	138.0	100.0	165.7

be termed "empathy" (*Einfuhlung*), and a comparative lack of these emotional qualities as they guided children other than their own. The emotional factor suggested to the experimenter as she observed mothers directing children other than their own was primarily a feeling of *responsibility* for the individual child.

Apparently Mothers II, IV, and IX, who were dominated by the feeling of sympathy and protection (expressed in a variety of ways), seemed to gain very little from their association with children other than their own. Mother II exhibited fear of the new and untried, which was not limited to her own child, but was demonstrated more frequently as she guided children in situations in which her child (G) was participating. Mother II attempted to overcome this characteristic, but she continued to be quickly

CHART I: PRACTICES OF THE ELEVEN MOTHERS TOWARD OWN CHILD AND TOWARD OTHER CHILDREN

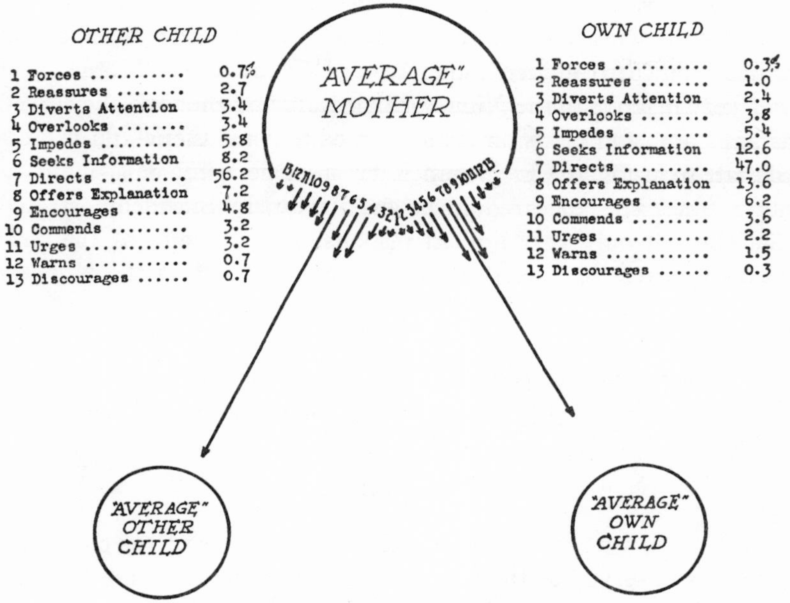
OTHER CHILD
1 Forces 0.7%
2 Reassures 2.7
3 Diverts Attention 3.4
4 Overlooks 3.4
5 Impedes 5.8
6 Seeks Information 8.2
7 Directs 56.2
8 Offers Explanation 7.2
9 Encourages 4.8
10 Commends 3.2
11 Urges 3.2
12 Warns 0.7
13 Discourages 0.7
"AVERAGE" MOTHER
OWN CHILD
1 Forces 0.3%
2 Reassures 1.0
3 Diverts Attention 2.4
4 Overlooks 3.8
5 Impedes 5.4
6 Seeks Information 12.6
7 Directs 47.0
8 Offers Explanation 13.6
9 Encourages 6.2
10 Commends 3.6
11 Urges 2.2
12 Warns 1.5
13 Discourages 0.3
"AVERAGE" OTHER CHILD
"AVERAGE" OWN CHILD

Scale: One-half inch = 10 per cent.

aroused by any unusual happenings and constantly placed restrictions upon G's activities. Mother IV concentrated her attention upon C, discriminating in the methods she chose in guiding C to the exclusion of other children. She exhibited indifference toward other children except those of her friends, and frequently seemed to resent the interests and activities initiated and participated in by J, E, and K, the more active and independent group. Mother IX expressed much concern over her child, I. Her other child, H, she apparently regarded with less interest. She exhibited at times an intolerant attitude toward the more aggressive and independent members of the group, J, E, and K. C, the child of a personal friend, and her own children were the principal recipients of Mother IX's guidance.

Other mothers, including Mothers I, III, V, VIII, X, and XI, were actively interested in the children participating in this group, and their guidance techniques revealed an honest attempt to help the individual learn as he or she solved personal and group problems. However, at times these six mothers exhibited more interest and a more sympathetic attitude toward their own children, a fact which seemed to influence their choice of practices. Mother VII was very inactive in the Nursery School during the time she served as assistant. On occasion she exhibited a sympathetic and protective attitude toward L and an interest in her problems, while at other times she appeared to be disinterested. She demonstrated that she felt only very limited responsibility for any of the children's progress and welfare as she made contacts in the Nursery School.

CHILDREN'S ACTIVITIES RECORDED AT THE TIME THE PRACTICES WERE USED BY THE MOTHERS IN ROUTINE AND NON-ROUTINE SITUATIONS

A detailed study was made by the experimenter of the children's activities observed at the time the various practices were used by the mothers in assisting the children in the routine and non-routine situations. A summary of the facts revealed by this detailed study is presented in Table V, based upon data found in the study of general trends[4] which show the frequency of the observance of each activity at the time the various practices were used by the mothers in assisting the children in routine and non-routine situations.

The total number of children's activities, 2,777, was observed at the time the mothers served as assistants. As shown in Table V, the largest number of children's activities, equaling 35.5 per cent of the total, was observed at the time *directs* was used by the mothers.

The second largest group of children's activities, 21.6 per cent of the total, occurred when the practice *seeks information* was used. Other practices listed in the order of frequency with which the children's activities were observed, were as follows: *offers explanation,* 13.3 per cent; *urges* and *impedes,* each 4.3 per cent;

[4] See footnote 2, page 51.

reassures, 3.8 per cent; *commends,* 2.7 per cent; *discourages* and *warns,* each 2.5 per cent; *encourages,* 1.8 per cent; *diverts attention,* 1.6 per cent; *forces,* 1.0 per cent; and *overlooks,* 0.8 per cent, were used at the time fewest activities were recorded.

In studying the types of children's activities and the frequency with which the various activities were observed at the time the different practices were used by the mothers, the experimenter found that certain significant facts were revealed. The results showed that the children *succeeded in carrying out the instructions of the mothers* approximately ten times as frequently as they *failed in carrying out the instructions.* Thirteen practices were used at the time the children were *successful in carrying out the mothers' instructions,* while only seven practices were used at the time children *failed in carrying out instructions.* The order of frequency with which the children *succeeded in carrying out instructions,* when grouped with the practices selected by the mothers in the same situations, showed that *directs* ranked first; *impedes,* second; *seeks information,* third; *urges,* fourth; *forces* and *warns,* fifth place; *offers explanation,* sixth; *reassures,* seventh; *encourages,* eighth; *diverts attention,* ninth; and *discourages,* tenth. *Commends,* next in rank, occupied the eleventh place, and *overlooks,* the practice used when the children's activities were described as *succeeds in carrying out instructions,* was recorded least frequently by observers in the Nursery School. The practices chosen by the mothers at the time the children's activities showed that they *failed in carrying out the mothers' instructions,* when listed in the order of frequency, were *seeks information, offers explanation, encourages, impedes, diverts attention,* and *discourages.* Seventy-four and six-tenths per cent of the activities classified as *failure in carrying out instructions* were observed at the same time that the mothers chose *directs* as a practice.

A study of the data revealed that the practice, *directs,* was selected relatively frequently by the mothers at the time the records showed the children were *successful in carrying out the mothers' instructions.* Furthermore, the records revealed that *directs* was observed with approximately the same frequency at the time the children's activities showed *failure in carrying out the*

DISTRIBUTION OF CHILDREN'S ACTIVITIES IN SITUATIONS

Children's Activities	No. of Activities	Seeks Information		Offers Explanation		Diverts Attention		Urges		Directs	
		No.	Per Cent	No.	Per Cent	No.	Per Cent	No.	Per Cent	No.	Per Cent
Succeeds in carrying out instructions ...	650	43	6.6	16	2.4	6	0.9	33	5.0	410	63.0
Fails to carry out instructions	63	5	7.9	3	4.7	1	1.5	..	...	47	74.6
Overlooks instructions	21	7	33.3	1	4.7	1	4.7	1	4.7	10	47.6
Solves problem with assistance	79	9	11.4	12	15.2	2	2.5	1	1.2	43	54.4
Does task independently	97	11	11.3	8	8.2	..	...	6	6.1	59	60.8
Requests assistance ..	17	2	11.7	..	...	..	...	..	...	9	52.9
Expresses inability to do task	25	9	36.0	3	12.0	..	...	..	...	10	40.0
Resists	15	2	13.3	..	...	..	...	..	...	11	73.3
Accepts assistance passively..........	183	22	12.0	13	7.1	..	...	5	2.7	130	71.0
Agrees to suggestion ..	201	59	29.3	54	26.8	7	3.4	12	5.9	22	10.9
Expresses insecurity ..	14	4	28.5	..	...	..	...	1	7.1	9	64.2
Demands property rights	5	1	20.0	..	...	..	...	..	...	4	80.0
Foregoes claim to property..........	2	1	50.0	..	...	..	...	..	...	..	....
Attacks child	6	..	...	..	...	..	...	..	...	4	66.6
Accepts material	1	..	...	..	...	1	100	..	...	..	....
Snatches toy	13	..	...	..	...	..	...	..	...	5	38.4
Expresses disapproval	42	5	11.9	12	28.5	1	2.3	..	...	17	40.4
Expresses interest ...	55	8	14.5	15	25.4	3	5.4	..	...	19	34.5
Requests information .	167	11	6.5	59	35.3	..	...	7	4.1	66	39.5
Gives information ...	275	253	92.0	3	1.0	2	0.8	1	0.4	9	3.2
Expresses a need	92	5	5.4	17	18.4	..	...	32	34.7	23	25.0
Offers explanation ...	88	7	7.9	27	30.6	1	1.0	3	3.4	32	36.3
Joins activity	14	2	14.2	2	14.2	..	...	3	21.4	4	28.5
Withdraws	56	4	7.1	12	21.4	2	3.5	2	3.5	19	33.9
Calls attention to self or to activity	59	5	8.5	6	10.1	3	5.0	2	3.3	23	38.9
Repeats	58	15	25.8	14	24.1	1	1.7	1	1.7	21	36.2
Cries	106	17	13.2	10	9.4	2	1.8	..	...	44	41.5
Laughs	12	3	25.0	2	16.6	3	25.0	..	...	..	....
Uses unintelligible language	36	..	...	13	36.1	6	16.6	..	...	12	33.3
No response	325	92	28.3	69	21.2	4	1.2	10	3.0	25	7.6
Total	2,777	602	21.6	371	13.3	46	1.6	120	4.3	1,087	35.5

V

IN WHICH PRACTICES OF THE MOTHERS WERE USED

Encourages		Impedes		Forces		Warns		Overlooks		Commends		Reassures		Discourages	
No.	Per Cent	No.	Per Cent	No.	Per Cent	No.	Per Cent	No.	Per Cent	No.	Per Cent	No.	Per Cent	No.	Per Cent
7	1.0	64	9.8	26	4.0	26	4.0	1	0.1	2	0.3	11	1.6	5	0.7
3	4.7	3	4.7	..	...	..	...	..	...	..	...	..	...	1	1.5
1	4.7	..	...	..	...	..	...	..	...	..	...	..	...	..	...
4	5.0	..	...	..	...	1	1.2	..	...	3	3.8	3	3.8	1	1.2
2	2.0	1	1.0	..	...	..	...	1	1.0	5	5.1	4	4.1	..	...
..	...	..	...	..	...	..	...	..	...	..	...	..	...	6	35.2
2	8.0	..	...	..	...	..	...	1	4.0	..	...	..	...	..	...
..	...	1	0.6	..	...	1	0.6	..	...	..	...	..	...	..	...
3	1.6	1	0.5	..	...	..	...	..	...	1	0.5	7	4.2	1	0.5
9	4.4	3	1.4	..	...	20	9.9	..	...	5	2.4	4	1.9	6	2.9
..	...	..	...	..	...	..	...	..	...	..	...	..	...	..	...
..	...	..	...	..	...	1	50.0	..	...	..	...	..	...	..	...
..	...	2	33.3	..	...	..	...	..	...	..	...	..	...	..	...
..	...	7	53.8	..	...	..	...	..	...	..	...	..	...	1	7.6
..	...	3	7.1	..	...	1	2.3	..	...	..	...	..	...	3	7.1
2	3.6	..	...	..	...	1	1.8	..	...	4	7.2	3	5.4	..	...
2	1.1	3	1.7	..	...	2	1.1	4	2.3	4	2.3	7	4.1	2	1.1
1	0.4	2	0.8	..	...	2	0.8	..	...	1	0.4	..	...	1	0.4
2	2.1	..	...	..	...	3	3.2	1	1.0	..	...	3	3.2	6	6.3
1	1.0	7	7.9	..	...	1	1.0	..	...	3	3.4	5	5.6	1	1.0
..	...	1	7.1	..	...	..	...	..	...	..	...	..	...	2	14.2
1	1.7	2	3.5	..	...	1	1.7	..	...	5	8.9	5	8.9	3	5.3
1	1.6	1	1.6	..	...	..	...	13	22.0	1	1.6	2	3.3	2	3.3
..	...	1	1.7	..	...	1	1.7	..	...	2	3.4	2	3.4	..	...
2	1.8	4	3.7	1	0.9	1	0.9	1	0.9	1	0.9	18	16.9	5	4.7
1	8.3	1	8.3	..	...	..	...	..	...	..	...	1	8.3	1	8.3
..	...	1	2.7	2	5.5	1	2.7	..	...	1	2.7	..	...	..	...
7	2.1	13	4.0	..	...	9	2.7	2	0.6	39	12.0	33	10.1	22	6.7
51	1.8	121	4.3	29	1.0	72	2.5	24	0.8	77	2.7	108	3.8	69	2.5

instructions of the mothers. The data failed to reveal the basis for these two types of behavior observed at the time the same practice was chosen. However, the experimenter's observation tended to support the probability that the children's behavior was in response to a series of factors and conditions not described in the data and that no one factor could be singled out and a relationship established with the children's behavior observed at approximately the same time that a given practice was directed toward an individual child or a group of children.

A comparison was made of the practices chosen at the times the children's activities were classified as *did the task independently, solved problems with assistance,* and *requested assistance.* In the first place, the activities of the group showed that they were able to solve their problems independently more frequently than they requested and received assistance. *Directs* was employed at the time 60.8 per cent of the children's activities were classified as exhibiting independence in the solution of problems. In addition, the following practices were recorded in the order of frequency with which independent behavior was recorded parallel with the use of the individual practices: *seeks information,* 11.3 per cent; *offers explanation,* 8.2 per cent; *urges,* 6.1 per cent; *commends,* 5.1 per cent; *reassures,* 4.1 per cent; *encourages,* 2.0 per cent; and *overlooks* and *impedes,* each 1.0 per cent. The problems were solved independently least frequently at the time *overlooks* and *impedes* were recorded. When the children's activities were classified as *solves problems with assistance* and *requests assistance,* 54.4 per cent of the former activities occurred when *directs* was used as a practice, and 52.9 per cent of the latter activities occurred when the same practice was employed.

When the children received assistance in the solution of problems, the following practices were observed, and the number of times they appeared in this activity recorded: *offers explanation,* 15.2 per cent; *seeks information,* 11.4 per cent; *encourages,* 5.0 per cent; *commends* and *reassures,* each 3.8 per cent; *diverts attention,* 2.5 per cent; and *urges, warns,* and *discourages* were each used 1.2 per cent of the total number of times the activity was described as *receiving assistance.* At the time the children *re-*

quested assistance, practices other than *directs* were observed, including *discourages*, 35.2 per cent, and *seeks information*, 11.7 per cent.

The experimenter chose to examine next certain other activities of the children as well as concurrent practices of the mothers. The following practices were observed at the time the children exhibited *resistance*. The record of *directs* showed that 73.3 per cent of the *resistant* behavior was observed at the time this practice was recorded. *Seeks information* accounted for 13.3 per cent of all *resistant* behavior, and 0.6 per cent of this same behavior was observed at the time that *impedes* and *warns* were each observed. At the time *combative* activities were observed in the children's records, two practices were chosen by the mothers: 66.6 per cent of the *combative* activities were shown in the records at the time *directs* was used, and 33.3 per cent of these activities occurred at the time *impedes* was selected. A large group of practices, including twelve of the thirteen, were chosen at the time *crying* was observed. The one practice not observed in this instance was *urges*. The children *cried* relatively frequently when the following practices were recorded, as is shown by the accompanying record of frequency with which *crying* occurred: *reassures*, 16.9 per cent; *seeks information*, 13.2 per cent; *offers explanation*, 9.4 per cent; *discourages*, 4.7 per cent. This behavior appeared relatively infrequently in the children's records with the use of the practices, *diverts attention, encourages, impedes, forces, warns, overlooks,* and *commends*.

Children's *laughter* accompanied seven of the mothers' practices somewhat infrequently. The seven practices included *seeks information, offers explanation, diverts attention, encourages, impedes, reassures,* and *discourages*.

Activities of the children which apparently influenced the mothers' selection of certain practices were the situations in which the children *requested information*; 59.0 per cent of those requests were observed at the time the mothers used the practice, *offers explanation*. Twenty-two per cent of the activities classified as *calling attention to self or activity* were observed at the time the practice, *overlooks*, appeared in the records.

In the instances of *no response*, the practices of the mothers were distributed among the situations as follows: *seeks information,* 28.3 per cent; *offers explanation,* 21.2 per cent; *commends,* 12.0 per cent; *reassures,* 10.1 per cent; *directs,* 7.6 per cent; *discourages,* 6.7 per cent; *impedes,* 4.0 per cent; *urges,* 3.0 per cent; *warns,* 2.7 per cent; *encourages,* 2.1 per cent; *diverts attention,* 1.2 per cent; and *overlooks,* 0.9 per cent.

A comparative analysis was made of the children's activities at the time the practices were used by their own mothers and at the time the same practices were used by the mothers of other children. The results of the analysis of the records are shown in Tables VI and VII.

The greatest number of the children's activities at the time their own mothers acted as assistants, and at the time other mothers served, were classified as *succeeds in carrying out instructions.* When each of the mothers supervised the activities of the children, from 62.7 per cent to 63.1 per cent of this activity was observed at the time *directs* was recorded. The analysis further showed the use of *impedes* at the time 9.3 per cent of the children's activities occurred; *warns,* when 5.0 per cent of the children's activities were observed; *urges,* 5.9 per cent; *encourages,* 2.5 per cent; *offers explanation,* 3.3 per cent; and *discourages,* 1.6 per cent. These percentages represent a greater proportion of the children's activities observed at the time the accompanying practices were used by their own mothers than when other mothers used the same practices. However, the records of the children showed this same activity, *succeeds in carrying out instructions,* grouped more frequently with other practices when these practices were used by other mothers. The practices in the above group included *seeks information,* 6.9 per cent, while the children's own mothers' records showed 5.0 per cent of this activity; *forces,* 4.6 per cent when their own mothers' records showed 0.8 per cent of their activities in comparable situations; and *reassures,* 2.0 per cent when other mothers used this practice and 0.8 per cent when their own mothers used the same practice. The mothers of other children were observed using the practices, *diverts attention, overlooks,* and *commends,* when the children's activity was described as *succeeds in carrying out instructions*, while the children's own mothers failed to use these practices at the time this activity was observed.

When the children's record of activities showed *failure in carrying out instructions*, the following practices of the mothers were observed and a record was made of the frequency with which each practice was used: 96.4 per cent of this activity was observed at the time their own mothers used the practice, *directs,* and 59.4 per cent at the time other mothers used the same practice; *seeks information* was recorded when 3.8 per cent of the children's activities were classified as *failure in carrying out instructions* at the time their own mothers were present, and 10.8 per cent of this activity was observed when other mothers used this same practice. The children's own mothers were observed using the two practices, *directs* and *seeks information,* at the time the children's activities indicated that they had *failed in carrying out instructions,* while other mothers' records showed the use of *offers explanation, diverts attention, encourages, impedes,* and *discourages.*

When the children's behavior was classified as *resistant,* their own mothers were observed using the two practices, *seeks information* and *directs,* and other mothers' records included the two practices listed above and, in addition, *offers explanation, encourages,* and *overlooks.*

The activities of the children which seemed to influence the type of practice used by their own mothers and by mothers of other children were *requests information* and *gives information.* The children *requested information* most frequently at the time the mothers' practices were classified as *offers explanation*; and when the children's activities were classified as *gives information,* the mothers used the practice, *seeks information,* with comparable frequency.

When *crying* was observed most frequently, the practices used by the mothers were *directs* and *reassures,* as shown in the records of both groups. This behavior was observed least frequently when *seeks information, offers explanation, encourages, impedes,* and *discourages* appeared as practices in the records of both groups of mothers. In addition, mothers of other children were observed

TABLE

Distribution of Children's Activities in Situations in Which

Children's Activities	No. of Activities		Seeks Information		Offers Explanation		Diverts Attention		Urges		Directs	
	No.	Per Cent	No.	Per Cent	No.	Per Cent	No.	Per Cent	No.	Per Cent	No.	Per Cent
Succeeds in carrying out instructions ..	118	17.6	6	5.0	4	3.3	..	...	7	5.9	74	62.7
Fails to carry out instructions	26	4.1	1	3.8	..	...	..	...	..	...	25	96.1
Overlooks instructions	8	1.2	2	25.0	..	...	..	...	..	...	6	75.0
Solves problem with assistance	9	1.3	..	...	2	22.2	..	...	..	...	7	77.7
Does task independently	10	1.4	1	10.0	..	...	..	...	..	...	6	60.0
Requests assistance	12	1.7	1	8.3	..	...	..	...	..	...	5	41.6
Expresses inability to do the task ...	2	0.3	1	50.0	..	...	..	...	..	...	1	50.0
Resists	4	0.5	1	25.0	..	...	..	...	..	...	2	50.0
Accepts assistance passively	29	4.4	2	6.8	1	3.4	..	...	..	...	26	89.6
Agrees to suggestion	42	6.3	10	23.8	13	30.9	2	4.7	1	2.3	8	19.0
Expresses insecurity	6	0.9	..	...	..	...	..	...	1	16.6	5	83.3
Demands property rights	3	0.4	1	33.0	..	...	..	...	..	...	2	67.0
Foregoes claim to property	..	...	..	...	..	...	..	...	..	...	..	....
Attacks child	1	0.1	..	...	..	...	..	...	..	...	..	....
Accepts material ..	1	0.1	..	...	..	...	1	100	..	...	..	....
Snatches toy	3	0.4	..	...	..	...	..	...	..	...	1	33.0
Expresses disapproval	16	2.3	2	12.5	4	25.0	..	...	..	...	5	31.2
Expresses interest ..	8	1.2	..	...	5	62.5	..	...	..	...	2	25.0
Requests infortion	56	8.4	5	8.9	24	42.8	..	...	..	...	17	30.3
Gives information ..	63	9.5	60	95.2	..	...	2	3.1	..	...	1	1.5
Expresses a need ...	45	6.6	3	6.6	11	24.4	..	...	..	...	20	44.4
Offers explanation .	47	6.8	1	2.1	12	25.5	..	...	..	...	22	46.8
Joins activity	4	0.5	..	...	1	25.0	..	...	..	...	3	75.0
Withdraws	16	2.4	1	6.2	2	12.5	1	6.2	..	...	6	37.5
Calls attention to self or to activity	26	4.1	3	11.5	2	7.6	..	...	..	...	10	38.4
Repeats	13	1.9	2	15.3	3	23.0	1	7.6	..	...	6	46.0
Cries	27	4.0	2	7.4	4	14.8	..	...	..	...	9	33.3
Laughs	5	0.8	1	20.0	2	40.0	..	...	..	...	..	....
Uses unintelligible language	10	1.4	..	...	3	30.0	..	...	..	...	5	50.0
No response	62	9.3	11	17.7	14	22.5	1	1.6	2	2.9	6	9.6
Total	672	...	117	17.4	107	15.9	8	1.1	11	1.6	280	41.6

VI

THE CHILDREN'S OWN MOTHERS USED THE VARIOUS PRACTICES

En-courages		Impedes		Forces		Warns		Overlooks		Commends		Reassures		Dis-courages	
No.	Per Cent	No.	Per Cent	No.	Per Cent	No.	Per Cent	No.	Per Cent	No.	Per Cent	No.	Per Cent	No.	Per Cent
3	2.5	14	11.8	1	0.8	6	5.0	..	...	..	...	1	0.8	2	1.6
..	...	..	...	..	...	..	...	..	...	..	...	..	...	..	...
..	...	..	...	..	...	..	...	..	...	..	...	..	...	..	...
..	...	..	...	..	...	..	...	..	...	..	...	..	...	..	...
1	10.0	..	...	..	...	..	...	..	...	..	...	2	20.0	..	...
..	...	..	...	..	...	..	...	..	...	..	...	..	...	6	50.0
..	...	..	...	..	...	1	25.0	..	...	..	...	..	...	..	...
..	...	..	...	..	...	..	...	..	...	..	...	..	...	..	...
..	...	..	...	..	...	..	...	..	...	..	...	..	...	..	...
3	7.1	..	...	..	...	1	2.3	..	...	1	2.3	3	7.1	..	...
..	...	..	...	..	...	..	...	..	...	..	...	..	...	..	...
..	...	..	...	..	...	..	...	..	...	..	...	..	...	..	...
..	...	1	100	..	...	..	...	..	...	..	...	..	...	..	...
..	...	2	67.0	..	...	..	...	..	...	..	...	..	...	..	...
..	...	1	6.2	..	...	1	6.2	..	...	2	12.5	..	...	3	18.7
..	...	..	...	..	...	..	...	..	...	..	...	..	...	..	...
2	3.5	1	1.7	..	...	1	1.7	1	1.7	1	1.7	3	5.3	1	1.7
..	...	..	...	..	...	..	...	..	...	..	...	..	...	..	...
1	2.2	..	...	..	...	1	2.2	1	2.2	..	...	2	4.4	6	13.4
..	...	5	10.6	..	...	1	2.1	..	...	1	2.1	4	8.5	1	2.1
..	...	..	...	..	...	..	...	..	...	..	...	..	...	..	...
1	6.2	..	...	..	...	..	...	..	...	2	12.5	1	6.2	2	12.5
..	...	..	...	..	...	..	...	9	34.6	..	...	..	...	2	7.6
..	...	..	...	..	...	..	...	..	...	..	...	1	7.6	..	...
..	...	1	3.7	..	...	..	...	..	...	..	...	8	29.6	3	11.1
1	20.0	1	20.0	..	...	..	...	..	...	..	...	..	...	..	...
..	...	..	...	2	20.0	..	...	..	...	..	...	..	...	..	...
2	2.9	3	4.8	..	...	1	1.6	2	2.9	4	6.4	7	11.2	9	14.5
14	2.0	29	4.3	3	0.4	13	1.9	13	1.9	10	1.4	32	4.7	35	5.2

TABLE

DISTRIBUTION OF CHILDREN'S ACTIVITIES IN SITUATIONS

Children's Activities	No. of Activities		Seeks Information		Offers Explanation		Diverts Attention		Urges		Directs	
	No.	Per Cent	No.	Per Cent	No.	Per Cent	No.	Per Cent	No.	Per Cent	No.	Per Cent
Succeeds in carrying out instructions	532	20.3	37	6.9	12	2.2	6	1.1	26	4.8	336	63.1
Fails to carry out instructions	37	1.8	4	10.8	3	8.1	1	2.7	..	...	22	59.4
Overlooks instructions	13	0.6	5	38.4	1	7.6	1	7.6	1	7.6	4	30.7
Solves problem with assistance	70	3.3	9	12.8	10	14.2	2	2.8	1	1.4	36	51.4
Does task independently	87	4.1	10	11.4	8	9.2	..	...	6	6.9	53	60.9
Requests assistance	5	0.2	1	20.0	..	...	..	...	..	...	4	80.0
Expresses inability to do the task ..	23	1.0	8	34.8	3	13.0	..	...	..	...	9	39.1
Resists	11	0.5	1	9.0	..	...	..	...	..	...	9	81.8
Accepts assistance passively	154	7.4	20	12.9	12	7.8	..	...	5	3.2	104	67.5
Agrees to suggestion	159	7.6	49	30.8	41	25.7	5	3.1	11	6.9	14	8.8
Expresses insecurity	8	0.3	4	50.0	..	...	..	...	..	...	4	50.0
Demands property rights	2	0.1	..	...	..	...	..	...	..	...	2	100
Foregoes claim to property	2	0.1	1	50.0	..	...	..	...	..	...	..	...
Attacks child	5	0.2	..	...	..	...	..	...	..	...	4	80.0
Accepts material ..	..	...	..	...	..	...	..	...	..	...	..	...
Snatches toy	10	0.4	..	...	..	...	..	...	..	...	4	40.0
Expresses disapproval	26	1.3	3	11.5	8	30.7	1	3.8	..	...	12	46.1
Expresses interest .	47	2.2	8	17.0	10	21.2	3	6.3	..	...	17	36.1
Requests information	111	5.3	6	5.4	35	32.4	..	...	7	6.3	49	44.1
Gives information .	212	10.1	193	91.0	3	1.4	..	...	1	0.4	8	3.7
Expresses a need ..	47	2.2	2	4.2	6	12.7	..	...	32	68.0	3	6.3
Offers explanation	41	2.0	6	14.6	15	36.5	1	2.4	3	7.3	10	24.3
Joins activity	10	0.4	2	20.0	1	10.0	..	...	3	30.0	1	10.0
Withdraws	40	2.0	3	7.5	10	25.0	1	2.5	2	5.0	13	32.5
Calls attention to self or to activity	33	1.5	2	6.0	4	12.1	3	9.0	2	6.0	13	39.3
Repeats	45	2.2	13	28.8	11	24.4	..	...	1	2.2	15	33.3
Cries	79	3.7	15	18.9	6	7.6	2	2.5	..	...	35	44.3
Laughs	7	0.3	2	28.5	..	...	3	42.8	..	...	..	...
Uses unintelligible language	26	1.3	..	...	10	38.4	6	23.0	..	...	7	26.9
No response	263	12.6	81	30.8	55	20.9	3	1.1	8	3.0	19	7.2
Total	2,105	...	485	23.0	264	12.0	38	1.8	109	5.1	807	38.3

VII

<small>IN WHICH OTHER MOTHERS USED THE VARIOUS PRACTICES</small>

En-courages		Impedes		Forces		Warns		Overlooks		Commends		Reassures		Dis-courages	
No.	Per Cent	No.	Per Cent	No.	Per Cent	No.	Per Cent	No.	Per Cent	No.	Per Cent	No.	Per Cent	No.	Per Cent
4	0.7	50	9.3	25	4.6	20	3.7	1	0.2	2	0.4	10	2.0	3	0.5
3	8.1	3	8.1	..	...	..	...	..	...	..	...	..	...	1	2.7
..	...	..	...	..	...	..	...	..	...	..	...	..	...	..	...
4	5.7	..	...	..	...	1	1.4	..	...	3	4.2	3	4.2	1	1.4
1	1.1	1	1.1	..	...	..	...	1	1.1	5	5.7	2	2.3	..	...
..	...	..	...	..	...	..	...	..	...	..	...	..	...	..	...
2	8.7	..	...	..	...	..	...	1	4.3	..	...	..	...	..	...
..	...	1	9.0	..	...	..	...	..	...	..	...	..	...	..	...
3	1.9	1	0.6	..	...	..	...	..	...	1	0.6	7	4.5	1	0.6
6	3.7	3	1.8	..	...	19	11.9	..	...	4	2.5	1	0.6	6	3.7
..	...	..	...	..	...	..	...	..	...	..	...	..	...	..	...
..	...	..	...	..	...	..	...	..	...	..	...	..	...	..	...
..	...	..	...	..	...	1	50.0	..	...	..	...	..	...	..	...
..	...	1	20.0	..	...	..	...	..	...	..	...	..	...	..	...
..	...	..	...	..	...	..	...	..	...	..	...	..	...	..	...
..	...	5	50.0	..	...	..	...	..	...	..	...	..	...	1	10.0
..	...	2	7.6	..	...	..	...	..	...	..	...	..	...	..	...
2	4.2	..	...	..	...	1	2.3	..	...	3	6.3	3	6.3	..	...
..	...	2	1.8	..	...	1	0.9	3	2.7	3	2.7	4	3.6	1	0.9
1	0.4	2	0.9	..	...	2	0.9	..	...	1	0.4	..	...	1	0.4
1	2.1	..	...	..	...	2	4.2	..	...	..	...	1	2.1	..	...
1	2.4	2	4.8	..	...	..	...	..	...	2	4.8	1	2.4	..	...
..	...	1	10.0	..	...	..	...	..	...	..	...	..	...	2	20.0
..	...	2	5.0	..	...	1	2.5	..	...	3	7.5	4	10.0	1	2.5
1	3.0	1	3.0	..	...	..	...	4	12.1	1	3.0	2	6.0	..	...
..	...	1	2.2	..	...	1	2.2	..	...	2	4.4	1	2.2	..	...
2	2.5	3	3.8	1	1.2	1	1.2	1	1.2	1	1.2	10	12.6	2	2.5
..	...	..	...	..	...	..	...	..	...	..	...	1	14.2	1	14.2
..	...	1	3.8	..	...	1	3.8	..	...	1	3.8	..	...	..	...
5	1.9	10	3.8	..	...	8	3.0	..	...	35	13.3	26	9.8	13	4.9
37	1.7	92	4.3	26	1.2	59	2.7	11	0.5	67	3.1	76	3.6	34	1.6

using the practices, *forces, warns, overlooks,* and *commends,* at the time the children *cried.*

At the time the children *failed to respond,* the practices used by each group of mothers were classified in a variety of categories; and the activities occurred with approximate frequency when each of these practices was used by members of both groups of assisting mothers.

A comparison of the practices used by the children's own mothers with those used by other mothers at the time the children were observed engaging in certain activities revealed the fact that the presence of the other mothers induced a greater variety of practices. There were several factors which seemed to influence mothers, in guiding children other than their own, to introduce frequently more than one practice into the situation; however, the data were inadequate for proving the presence of these factors. The mothers constantly revealed the lack of confidence in their guidance techniques as they directed other children. This group, as a whole, which had had limited training in understanding children's behavior, was inexperienced in guiding children other than their own, which fact apparently explained the basis for their lack of confidence in their own methods of guidance. Consequently, they habitually overlooked the importance of basing their successive practices upon the child's responses. Many times the experimenter observed that the mothers, in understanding and responding to requests, failed to take into account the individual differences of children. As pointed out by the experimenter, the characteristics described above were exhibited by the mothers in the number and the type of practices that they directed toward children other than their own.

Another factor which the experimenter observed was a failure on the part of the mothers to adopt the practice of securing a child's attention before attempting to change his interests and activities.

The mothers demonstrated improvement in their guidance techniques, and some of the factors described above were not observed as frequently at the close of the year as at the time the records were made for this study.

The activities of the children observed at the time their own mothers were present were compared with the activities of the same group at the time mothers other than their own were assisting. The results were tabulated and were presented in Tables VI and VII. The children were observed participating more frequently in the following activities at the time their own mothers were assistants in the Nursery School: *fails in carrying out instructions, overlooks instructions, requests assistance, expresses insecurity, demands property rights, accepts materials, expresses disapproval, requests information, offers explanation, joins activity, expresses a need, withdraws, calls attention to self or activity, cries, laughs,* and *uses unintelligible language.* Certain activities were observed to occur more frequently at the time the children were directed by mothers other than their own. These activities included the following: *succeeds in carrying out instructions, solves problem with assistance, does task independently, expresses inability to do task, accepts assistance passively, agrees to suggestion, foregoes claim to property, attacks child, expresses interest, gives information, repeats,* and *makes no response.*

Two activities observed with the same frequency when both groups of mothers were assistants were *resists* and *snatches a toy.* The only activity not recorded at the time the children's own mothers were assistants was the one in which the child *gave up his claim to property.* The children failed to *accept materials* at the time a mother other than their own had the responsibility of assisting in the Nursery School. They showed a preference for a greater diversity of activities at the time their own mothers were present than when other mothers were present.

ACTIVITIES OF THE CHILDREN IN ROUTINE AND NON-ROUTINE SITUATIONS

Records of the children's activities observed in the four routine and four non-routine situations were studied to find out the activities of each of the children in each of the situations.

The children's records showed that they were *successful in carrying out instructions* more frequently in the *mid-morning lunch* situation than in any other; in this situation their successful activities showed 35.4 per cent. In each of the routine situations, their records showed that the largest proportions of their activities were successful, ranging from the *mid-morning lunch* to the *care of wraps and exchange of clothing*, in which 22.4 per cent of the activities were successful. The frequency with which the children's activities were classed as *successful in carrying out instructions* in the non-routine situations showed limited differences in the various situations. This type of activity was shown with greatest frequency in the *instructional* period, with 16.9 per cent of their activities included in this classification; 16.7 per cent in *emergency* situations; 13.3 per cent in *conflicts*; and 12.9 per cent in *free play* situations.

In a study of the distribution and frequency with which the children's records showed they *failed in carrying out instructions* in each of the situations, it was apparent that this group failed less frequently than they succeeded in each of the situations. The instances of *failure in carrying out instructions* were recorded the greatest number of times in the *rest* situation, and least frequently in the *care of wraps and exchange of clothing* situation. The routine situations showed the following distribution of failure: in *rest* situations, 1.5 per cent; *toileting*, 1.1 per cent; and *care of wraps and exchange of clothing*, 0.4 per cent; no record of this activity was made in the *mid-morning lunch* situation. *Failure in carrying out instructions* was shown relatively infrequently in the non-routine situations. For example, in *emergency* situations, 0.6 per cent of the children's activities were classified in this group; in *instruction*, 0.6 per cent; in *free play*, 0.3 per cent; and this activity was not recorded at the time *conflicts* in the group were observed.

A comparison was made of the distribution of the children's behavior in which they *showed independence in doing the task* and in which they *requested assistance*. They showed a greater frequency of independence in the *rest* situation than in any other of the eight situations: 11.7 per cent of the children's activities in the *rest* situation were classified as *doing the task independently*; and in *conflict* situations, where this activity occurred least frequently, 1.1 per cent of the group's activities were listed under this classification. The records of the children in the remaining six situations indicated independence as follows: *toileting,* 7.5 per cent; *free play,* 5.3 per cent; *mid-morning lunch,* 4.2 per cent; *care of wraps and exchange of clothing,* 3.8 per cent; *instruction,* 3.3 per cent; and *emergency,* 2.0 per cent.

The children's records showed that they *requested assistance* in six of the eight situations, listed below in the order of frequency with which the records showed this activity: *free play,* 3.3 per cent; *conflicts,* 2.2 per cent; *care of wraps and exchange of clothing,* 1.6 per cent; *rest,* 1.0 per cent; *instruction,* 0.9 per cent; and *toileting,* 0.6 per cent. This activity was not recorded at the time the children were observed in *emergency* situations and in *mid-morning lunch* situations as revealed by the distribution of *doing the task independently* in each of the situations.

It was apparent that one or the other of certain activities was inevitable in a limited number of situations, as was shown when the *children demanded their property rights* and in the *foregoing of claims to property* in the same situations, including *free play, instructional,* and *conflict* situations. However, these activities were not limited to any individual child's record in the three situations, but were distributed in the records of B, E, J, K, G, H, and I.

The children's records showed that one child *attacked another* in the *toileting* situation, in the *instructional* periods, and in the *free play* and *conflict* situations. *Interest was expressed* by individuals in all of the situations included in this study. *Crying* was distributed in the records of the fourteen children throughout the eight situations; however, this behavior occurred most frequently in the *emergency* situations and least frequently in the *toileting* situations.

The children *expressed a need* in the following situations, listed in the order of frequency: *conflicts,* 7.7 per cent; *free play,* 6.3 per cent; *instruction,* 2.7 per cent; *mid-morning lunch,* 2.1 per cent; *rest,* 2.0 per cent; *emergency,* 2.0 per cent; *toileting,* 1.3 per cent; and *care of wraps and exchange of clothing,* 1.2 per cent.

SUMMARY

1. Among the thirteen practices analyzed in this chapter, the practice designated as *directs* occurred with the greatest frequency, both in the composite records of the group and in the records of the individual mothers. *Directs* constituted 51.8 per cent of the total number of practices.

2. The remaining twelve practices fell roughly into groups of two, each one of which closely paralleled the other in frequency of use. These six pairs, in the order of frequency with which they occurred in the mothers' records, were as follows: *seeks information* and *offers explanation, impedes* and *encourages, overlooks* and *commends, diverts attention* and *urges, reassures* and *warns, discourages* and *forces.*

3. All of the thirteen practices were used by seven of the eleven mothers. Each mother's record revealed differences in the frequency with which the practices were selected. The practices described as *forces* and *discourages* were limited to seven records.

4. Mother I directed the children most frequently, using 477 practices, while Mother II directed least frequently, using 211 practices during comparable observation periods.

5. *Directs* was observed with the greatest frequency in the individual mothers' records, ranging from 57.8 per cent in Mother IV's record to 39.8 per cent in Mother V's record. The distribution of the remaining practices followed closely the distribution of these practices in the aggregate records of the mothers.

6. The mothers assisted in the routine and non-routine situations in the following order, as shown by the number of situations in which they were participants: *mid-morning lunch, toileting, free play, care of wraps and exchange of clothing, instruction, emergency, rest,* and *conflicts.*

7. The results of this study revealed that the mothers selected all of the practices in the *toileting, free play,* and *instructional* situations.

8. The practices, *seeks information, offers explanation, urges, directs, encourages, impedes,* and *overlooks,* were selected by individuals in each of the routine and non-routine situations.

9. When practices used in each of the situations were compared, the results indicated that the mothers selected certain practices in five of the situations. The records showed the omission of the following practices in the various situations: In the *care of wraps and exchange of clothing*, the practices, *forces* and *discourages*, were not observed; three practices, *diverts attention, reassures,* and *discourages*, were not selected during the *midmorning lunch* periods; the practices recorded during *rest* periods did not include *warns*; the mothers did not use *commends* and *discourages* in *emergency* situations; and in situations in which *conflicts* occurred, the mothers indicated a preference for ten practices and did not select *warns, discourages,* and *reassures*.

10. Seven practices, *seeks information, offers explanation, diverts attention, directs, encourages, impedes,* and *overlooks*, were included in the records of each of the fourteen children.

11. The mothers indicated preferences for certain practices when directing children I, G, H, D, F, L, A, B, and Q. Children C, E, K, P, and J were each guided by all thirteen of the practices.

12. C's record revealed that she was guided most frequently of all of the fourteen children, as the mothers used 546 practices when directing C; and the other children's records were distributed between C's record and A's low record of 172 practices during comparable periods of time.

13. The children were each guided most frequently by the use of the practice, *directs,* which ranged from 61.8 per cent in Q's record to 33.7 per cent in A's record. A comparable frequency was observed in the guidance of each child in the selection of *encourages, impedes, seeks information,* and *offers explanation*.

14. A similarity was observed in the individuals' records in the infrequent use of three practices, *forces, reassures,* and *discourages*.

15. The results of this study showed that the presence of other mothers induced a greater variety of practices than those used by the children's own mothers at the time the children were engaged in certain activities.

16. The "average" mother in the group exhibited relatively more frequent use of the practices, *overlooks, seeks information,*

offers explanation, encourages, commends, and *warns,* when directing her own child.

17. When directing children of other mothers, the "average" mother exhibited a relatively higher preference for the practices, *reassures, diverts attention, impedes, directs, urges, forces,* and *discourages.*

18. The largest group of children's activities observed at the time the mothers were assistants revealed that approximately one-fourth of all of the activities were classified as *successful in carrying out the mothers' instructions.*

19. The children's records indicated that they *succeeded in carrying out instructions* with approximately ten times the frequency with which they were observed *failing to carry out instructions.*

20. The records of the *mid-morning lunch* periods and *conflict* situations failed to show any *failures in carrying out instructions.*

21. An examination of the records of the individual children revealed approximately the same distribution of the activities classified as *successful in carrying out instructions* in each of the routine and non-routine situations.

22. Certain activities of the children were limited to specific situations. The activities, *demands property rights* and *foregoes claim to property,* were confined to *free play, conflict,* and *instructional* situations. The behavior described as *child attacks another* was observed in *toileting, instructional, free play,* and *conflict* situations. *Crying* was observed in all of the situations, but was recorded most frequently in *emergency* and *toileting.*

23. Six of the activities, *snatches a toy, accepts materials, expresses insecurity, attacks a child, demands property rights,* and *foregoes claim to property,* were limited to the records of three children. The remaining twenty-four activities were participated in by the fourteen children with approximately the same frequency.

24. The children participated in a greater number of activities when their own mothers were present than at the time other mothers were serving as assistants.

25. In addition to the results of the analysis and compilations of the data, certain conditions prevailing in the Nursery School, along with a selected group of factors, were described; and a brief description of the personal characteristics of a number of the children was presented to indicate the factors which apparently influenced the mothers in their methods of guidance. However, the data were inadequate in establishing these relationships.

Chapter V
LANGUAGE OF MOTHERS AND CHILDREN

A STUDY of the language used by each mother when she acted as assistant was made from the stenographic records of the three three-hour observation periods. A study of the number of words used by the children was based upon similar records which were also made during the three three-hour periods of observation assigned each mother.

NUMBER OF WORDS

Table VIII and Chart II show the total number of words used by the eleven mothers and by each mother in speaking to the children in the group observed. Also found in Table VIII and Chart II are data relating to the total number of words used by the fourteen children in speaking to the mother assisting and to children of the group during the three three-hour observations. The eleven mothers used 25,440 words during the three observation periods, and the fourteen children used 3,787 words in making verbal contacts at the time the observation records were made. Mother VI's record showed that she used the greatest number of words—a total of 3,283 words. The smallest number of words was used by Mother II, whose record showed a count of 1,750 words. Mother VIII ranked second in greatest number of words with a total of 2,765 words, and the other mothers assumed the following positions in order of the frequency with which they spoke to the children: Mother XI, 2,588; Mother IX, 2,500; Mother X, 2,487; Mother I, 2,400; Mother V, 2,037; Mother VII, 1,982; Mother III, 1,885; Mother IV, 1,763; and Mother II, 1,750.

The number of words used by the mothers as shown in Table VIII was compared with the number and the practices revealed in the mothers' records as shown in Table I. The record of Mother VI, who talked more freely than any other mother,

TABLE VIII

NUMBER OF WORDS USED BY MOTHERS AND CHILDREN DURING
OBSERVATION PERIODS

Mother	Total Number of Words Used by Mothers	Number of Words Used First Day by—		Number of Words Used Second Day by—		Number of Words Used Third Day by—		Total Number of Words Used by Children
		M*	C†	M*	C†	M*	C†	
I	2,400	890	105	697	69	813	73	247
II	1,750	406	57	784	163	560	105	325
III	1,885	605	87	630	114	650	175	376
IV	1,763	553	67	890	45	320	77	189
V	2,037	435	23	765	103	837	143	269
VI	3,283	1,500	97	900	103	883	280	480
VII	1,982	485	198	878	153	619	94	445
VIII	2,765	625	61	675	42	1,465	108	211
IX	2,500	612	73	806	115	1,082	57	245
X	2,487	1,082	130	1,104	110	301	97	337
XI	2,588	950	203	853	255	785	205	663
Total	25,440	8,143	1,101	8,982	1,272	8,315	1,414	3,787

* M=Mother. † C=Children.

showed that she directed the children less frequently than did Mothers I and VIII. Mother I, whose record revealed the greatest number of practices, was outranked by Mothers VI, VIII, XI, IX, and X in the number of words used. Mother VI's record showed that she used the practices, *seeks information* and *offers explanation*, most frequently of any mother in the group; on the other hand, Mother II, whose verbal expressions with the children were most limited of any of the eleven mothers, selected these two practices much more frequently than did Mothers VIII, XI, and IX, who talked relatively more often than did Mother II. The record of Mother II, who used the fewest oral expressions with the children, failed to reveal any practices or group of practices used most or least frequently.

The tabulation of the number of words indicated the relative amount of verbalization used by the mothers and the children and a comparison of records for each of the three days assigned each individual mother for observation. The results failed to reveal (1) any relationship between the acquaintance of mother and

CHART II: NUMBER OF WORDS USED BY MOTHERS AND
CHILDREN DURING OBSERVATION PERIODS

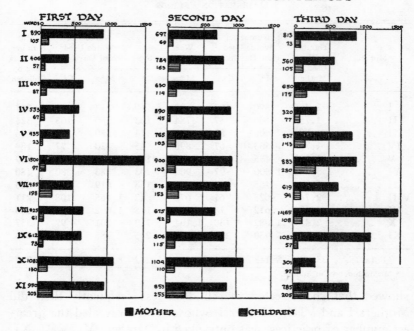

children and the amount of verbalization, or (2) any consistent influence of the amount of verbalization of either mother or children upon the verbal response of the other.

FORM OF SENTENCE STRUCTURE

Table IX and Chart III show the individual distribution of the three forms of sentence structure used by the group of mothers. A study of the use of the types of sentences indicated individual differences in the frequency with which the mothers used the sentences to convey their practices to the children, and no mother used only one type of sentence structure throughout the three observation periods. A comparison of the sentence structure used by the mothers and the amount of verbalization recorded for the children during the observation periods indicated no consistent relationship. Apparently the type of sentence, declarative, inter-rogative, or imperative, did not influence the mothers in the number of practices chosen, as no consistent relationship was established in comparing the frequency of the use of each type of sentence as shown in the observation records.

TABLE IX

NUMBER OF TIMES THE SENTENCE STRUCTURES WERE USED BY THE MOTHERS

Mother	Total Number of Sentences Used	Declarative Sentence	Interrogative Sentence	Imperative Sentence
I	197	73	62	62
II	124	50	36	38
III	126	39	44	43
IV	132	50	32	50
V	134	57	33	44
VI	223	97	62	64
VII	157	52	43	62
VIII	184	52	43	89
IX	163	53	48	62
X	183	53	37	93
XI	161	62	38	61
Total	1,784	638	478	668

The factor which apparently influenced the children in the amount of language they used was the length of time the children had been in the Nursery School before the mothers' records were made. Mothers XI, VI, and VII were among the last mothers to assist in the school. In each of their records the children are shown to have been relatively free in their verbal exchanges. Mothers I, VIII, and III assisted first in the group, and their recorded language indicates the opposite tendency with relation to the verbalization engaged in by the children. Hence this factor apparently outweighed other factors, such as the number of words used by the mothers, the structure of sentences chosen by the mothers to convey their directions to the children, and the mothers' previous contacts in the Nursery School when a comparison was made of the distribution of the children's oral expressions.

CHART III: FREQUENCY OF KINDS OF SENTENCES USED BY
MOTHERS WHILE UNDER OBSERVATION IN THE
NURSERY SCHOOL

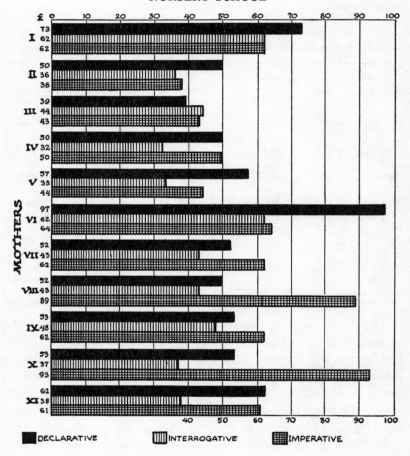

USE OF POSITIVE AND NEGATIVE SUGGESTIONS

The practices employed by the eleven mothers were classified in two groups—those practices in which positive suggestions were used by the mother, and those in which the mother directed by negative suggestions. The results of this classification for each individual mother are given in Table X.

TABLE X

MOTHERS' PRACTICES SHOWING USE OF POSITIVE AND NEGATIVE SUGGESTIONS

Mother	Total No. of Positive Suggestions	Per Cent of Positive Suggestions	Total No. of Negative Suggestions	Per Cent of Negative Suggestions	Total No. of Positive and Negative Suggestions
I	258	71	105	29	363
II	122	72	46	46	168
III	170	67	84	33	254
IV	157	74	55	26	212
V	131	67	65	33	196
VI	155	60	103	40	258
VII	154	63	91	37	245
VIII	228	60	152	40	380
IX	212	75	70	25	282
X	188	70	81	30	269
XI	134	55	109	45	243
Total .	1,909	..	961	..	2,870

Positive Suggestions. This term, as used here, applies to those practices by means of which the mother either directed the child in the choice of an acceptable activity or instructed him in the more constructive use of equipment.

Illustration. K is on the jungle gym with a broomstick in his hand. Mother III says, "Suppose you stand the broomstick in the corner, over here. Then you will have a chimney for your house." K replies, "I never thought of that."

Negative Suggestions. The term, *negative suggestion,* as used here, applies to those directions which either seemed intended to limit the child in his activity or called attention to an activity in which he was not to engage.

Illustration. Mother XI approaches P, who is crying, and says, "P, don't cry. Are you a cry-baby?" P answers, "No." Mother XI says, "Well, then, don't cry."

The records of this group of mothers showed that a markedly higher percentage of positive than of negative suggestions was used. The individuals chose positive suggestions varying in frequency from 75 per cent, as shown in Mother IX's record, to 55 per cent in Mother XI's record, showing a range of 20 per cent. The variation among the mothers in the use of negative suggestions was from 45 per cent in Mother XI's record to 25 per cent recorded at the time Mother IX was assisting. As in the case of positive suggestions, the variation among the mothers showed a range of 20 per cent.

When a comparison was made of the frequency of positive and negative suggestions with the amount of verbalization recorded for the children, it was discovered that apparently the use of positive and negative suggestions did not consistently encourage or discourage the children in orally expressing themselves.

TYPES OF CONVERSATION

As a matter of interest, a study was made of the unusual and interesting conversations engaged in by the mothers in directing the children in routine and play tasks. However, the data available for this part of the study were inadequate in establishing any definite relationship between the use of the language observed and the activities of the children.

The conversation of the mothers found in the records of the Nursery School was classified as follows and tabulated in Table XI.

1. *Echo.* By this type of conversation is meant the repetition by the mother of practically the same language used by the child.

Illustration. D says to Mother VIII, "I want to play with spoon." The mother replies, "You want to play with the spoon?"

Echo expressions were used by all the mothers, with the exception of Mother IV and Mother XI. Mother II used this type of conversation only once. Mother VI used it more frequently than any other mother in the group, her record showing the use of this form eleven times. The remaining seven mothers used this type of conversation occasionally, totaling twenty-nine times. The eleven mothers, considered as a unit, employed *echo* expressions forty-one times altogether.

2. *Rhyme. Rhymes* were used as a routine or play activity to suggest the problem to be solved. For example: "Thumb in the thumb place, fingers all together; this is the song we sing in mitten weather"; and, "See-saw, Margery Daw." This type of irrelevant conversation was employed by Mothers IV and IX, as shown in Table XI.

TABLE XI

EXPRESSIONS OBSERVED IN MOTHERS' CONVERSATION WITH CHILDREN

Type of Comment	MOTHER											
	I	II	III	IV	V	VI	VII	VIII	IX	X	XI	Total
Echo	2	1	4	..	3	11	8	7	4	1	..	41
Rhyme	..	..	..	1	..	..	..	..	1	..	..	2
Expression of approval	8	..	8	10	6	7	1	27	9	4	..	80
Polite phrase	..	..	..	6	3	5	6	5	1	5	..	31
Explanation	..	3	..	..	3	9	..	2	..	2	3	22
Question	2	1	1	..	..	..	1	1	..	..	..	6
Endearment	..	..	..	10	1	8	..	3	..	5	..	27
Total	12	5	13	27	16	40	16	45	15	17	3	209

3. *Expression of Approval.* The term *expression of approval* refers to those expressions which were apparently appended by the mother without any expressed relationship to what the child was doing, but with an implied connection with his activity.

Illustrations. G climbs the jungle gym. Mother III looks at G, who has reached the top, saying "That's lovely."

E has left the toilet. Mother VIII helps him fasten his coat, and says as E walks away, "That's a good boy."

Mothers II and XI omitted all expressions of this type of approval from their conversations with the children. Mother VII used such an expression once; Mother IV, four times; while Mother VIII used expressions of this type twenty-seven times. The remaining members of the group used detached expressions of approval from six to ten times each.

4. *Polite Phrases.* The term *polite phrases* refers to the language employed by the mother in her attempts to teach the child acceptable manners by coaching him in phrases.

> *Illustrations.* Mother X says to P, "P, say 'thank you' to D."
>
> F hands Mother VI a doll; Mother VI says, "Thank you, F." Mother VI returns doll to F and says, "Say 'thank you' to Mummy, F." F takes doll and walks away.

Polite phrases were used by Mothers IV, V, VI, VII, VIII, IX, and X, while Mothers I, II, III, and XI were not recorded as having used any expressions of this type. Mothers VII, IV, VI, VIII, and X, according to the records, apparently employed this type of phraseology in order to establish its use as a habit with the child.

Three other kinds of comments were noted in the records of the mothers as they associated with the children, and are described as follows: (1) *explanation* of equipment or objects in the environment which in no way were related to the task or activity at hand; (2) *questions* as to the child's information regarding some object not related to the given problem; and (3) *terms of endearment*. The distribution of these types of conversation is shown in Table XI.

> *Illustrations.* "See that can? It is used for watering flowers."
> "What color is your suit?"
> "Dear," "Sweet," "Darling."

These types of comment were of much less frequent occurrence than those types of conversation described as *expression of approval, rhyme,* and *echo.*

Five of the eleven mothers, Mothers I, III, IV, VII, and IX, offered no explanations, and of the remaining mothers who made offered explanations, only Mother VI made more than two or three. The total for the entire group was twenty-two for this type of comment. Five mothers put to the children questions of the type described—four mothers, one question each, and one, two questions, making a total of six such questions.

The records show that each mother used terms of endearment principally with her own child. Mother IV used such terms ten times, seven of which were with her own child. Mother VI used endearing expressions eight times, all, with but one exception, addressed to her own child. Mother V employed such terms once; Mother VIII, three times; and Mother XI, five times. The total number of such terms of endearment used by the mothers as a group was twenty-seven.

Mothers V and X used the word, "Silly," when they spoke disparagingly of their children's activities. This expression was used in situations where the child's behavior apparently caused the mother embarrassment, or when the child continued to cry after the mother had tried methods of appeasement.

DISCUSSION

A study of the mothers' language records indicated the following trends: (1) the mothers' familiarity with children in the group, and with the routine and play activities in which the children were interested, apparently did not consistently influence the individuals in the frequency with which they made verbal contacts with the children when acting as assistants; (2) mothers who made frequent verbal contacts with the children were inclined to talk freely with the children on all occasions; (3) mothers, as a rule, talked with greater freedom in situations where they had definite responsibilities, particularly in routine and instructional situations; (4) the repetition of set and standardized expressions, apparently the result of trying to establish habits in the child, were common to all mothers.

The following interesting tendencies were noted in the children's attempts at adjustment to the language habits of the mothers: (1) a capacity to respond acceptably to a variety of language patterns; (2) no consistent relationship established in the frequency with which the child responded to the variety of verbal expressions used by the mothers; (3) habits of response to the mothers' verbal contacts, as indicated by the frequency with which the children orally expressed themselves; (4) an interest in the conversation of adults, sometimes apparently for the sake of verbal exchange, and sometimes in so far as the expression responded to the child's need.

SUMMARY

1. In the number of words used by the mothers during the nine hours of observation, the records showed a variation ranging from 3,283 words recorded at the time Mother VI was observed to 1,750 words in Mother II's observation records.

2. Equally wide variation was found in the number of words used by the children at the time the mothers were assistants. The greatest number of words, 663, was recorded for the children at the time Mother XI was assisting, and the fewest words, 189, were used at the time Mother IV was present.

3. The records for the three observation periods failed to show the children's familiarity with the mothers as a condition determining the frequency with which they spoke to the mothers.

4. A comparison of the frequency of the use of declarative, interrogative, and imperative sentence structures with the amount of verbalization used by the children did not indicate any consistent relationship.

5. No relationship appeared between the use of positive and negative suggestions by the mothers and the number of words spoken by the children.

6. The number of words observed in the mothers' records and the type of sentences chosen by them failed to reveal any relationship with the frequency with which the individuals directed the children or the type of practices selected.

7. The length of time the children had been associated apparently was an important factor in the frequency with which the children expressed themselves verbally, as shown in the comparison of the mothers' records with the order in which the records were made at the time the mothers were assistants in the Nursery School.

Chapter VI
A STUDY OF SIX TYPES OF BEHAVIOR OBSERVED IN THE CHILDREN'S CONTACTS WITH ONE ANOTHER

In order to provide a basis for analysis of the six forms of behavior arbitrarily selected for study by the experimenter, one observation record of each child was made prior to the week that the child's mother participated in the Nursery School, one while she was assisting, and a third following her assignment. The records so obtained were then examined to determine the number and frequency with which the behavior traits were shown in the contacts made by the children.[1] The contacts showing these forms of behavior traits were classified under six headings, each descriptive of the overt behavior shown in a particular contact.

CLASSES OF BEHAVIOR IN CHILDREN'S CONTACTS

Co-operation.[2] This describes the contacts of the children in which their activities showed that the participants assumed joint responsibility in the development of a play interest or the solution of a problem, or shared voluntarily or upon request the use of play equipment or play materials.

Situation. E climbs into wagon. E says to J, "Come on, J; we are going to Southport." J climbs into the wagon and says, "I am going to Southport. I have a little baby to take care of." E says, "Goodbye, everybody. I hope to see you again. I am going to my friends." E steers the wagon as they ride around the yard, by

[1] *Contacts* is here defined as verbal or physical exchanges with another child or with a group of children.

[2] *Co-operation* was differentiated from *initiation of activity* by the differences in behavior shown by the child. If he accepted the responsibilities of an activity undertaken for the good of two or more in the group, his contact was classified as *co-operation*. If, however, the child originated the idea that promoted an activity in which other children participated, the contact was classified as *initiation of activity*.

holding on to the tongue of the wagon, and J pushes the wagon with one foot, holding on to the side of the wagon with one hand. E stops the wagon, gets out, and picks up the broom.

Initiation of Activity. This term comprises those activities of the child which show (1) independence in developing a group activity, (2) leadership in the solution of a problem in a group contact, (3) the use of pertinent and acceptable suggestions in the improvement of group play, and (4) the development of a play activity from a group interest.

Situation. E looks at camera, then picks up broom handle and says, "Oh, here's one." E lets the broom handle drag on the ground and marches around the yard saying, "Here comes the soldier," hitting the stick on the ground as he marches. J and K follow E, singing and marching.

Aggressiveness[3] is used as a term comprising the following activities of the children: self-assertiveness, demanding attention from the group by giving commands, grabbing or taking toys or play materials without the owner's consent, and the child's demanding that his wishes be accepted.

Situation. J goes to H, takes hold of the camera and says, "I need it." "That's mine." H holds on to the camera. J says, "Could I have it now?" H says, "No," and turns away.

Resistance. This term is used to describe contacts in which the child in his activities showed an unwillingness to obey a verbal request or demand, as indicated by withdrawal when approached by another child; refusal to discontinue an activity when interrupted or opposed by another person, or when any change was suggested in an activity; and by crying or other forms of opposition to verbal or physical stimulus, such as saying, "Don't," "No," "I won't."

Situation. P comes out of the toy house, goes to doll carriage and holds handle. J fixes doll covers in carriage. J takes hold of handle. P screams and holds to handle. J says, "I had it first." P holds the handle and screams. J pushes carriage and P follows, crying. P leaves the carriage.

[3] The positive activities of this type of behavior are classified under *initiation of activity.*

Combativeness. This term includes the contacts in which the child, either as defender or aggressor, makes an attack upon another child by slapping, kicking, knocking, or striking with something.

Situation. E comes out of toy house and picks up broom. E carries broom to sandbox and hits F, who is playing in the sandbox, with the broom. E says to F, "That's mine, don't you know? I am going to take you to my home. It's a very nice home. There are toys and everything." F walks away.

Resourcefulness. This encompasses those contacts in which the child showed independence in the management of equipment in routine situations, or in the use of play material or play equipment in unusual ways to express his interest or experience.

Situation. E walks to jungle gym and climbs up. J follows him. K pulls at rug on corner of jungle gym and says, "I am going to make mine dark. I am making a house. You can live with me." K spreads the rug over corner of jungle gym, placing the sides of the rug, and says, "This is the door. You have to bend down to get into the house. This way." K goes under the rug. K climbs down and goes and gets long pole. K stands the pole in the corner of the jungle gym and says, "See, J. Look, that is the chimney."

The fourteen children participated in 2,456 contacts, as shown in Table XII, in which one or more of the six forms of behavior were observed during the three three-hour observation periods assigned each child. In a study of the frequency with which the group showed each of the behaviors, the experimenter found that *resistance* was present in their contacts more often than any of the other forms of behavior. Twenty-seven and two-tenths per cent of the contacts that were studied were classified as *resistance*, 26.5 per cent as *co-operation*, 21.6 per cent as *aggressiveness*, and 15.1 per cent as *initiation of activity*. The types of activities observed least frequently in this group of contacts were *resourcefulness* and *combativeness*, which appeared in 7.0 per cent and 2.6 per cent, respectively, of the 2,456 children's contacts.

The behavior of the individual child was studied in the 2,456 contacts, and a tabulation was made of the number of times each of the six behavior traits was overtly shown in a child's contacts

TABLE XII

Total Number and Frequency with Which Each of the Six Classes of Behavior Was Overtly Shown in the Children's Contacts

Child	Total Number of Contacts*	Co-operation		Resistance		Aggressiveness		Combativeness		Initiation of Activity		Resourcefulness	
		Number	Per Cent	Number	Per Cent	Number	Per Cent	Number	Per Cent	Number	Per Cent	Number	Per Cent
A	148	30	20.3	46	31.1	40	27.1	4	2.7	17	11.4	11	7.4
B	154	36	23.3	52	33.8	42	27.3	3	1.9	17	11.1	4	2.6
C	211	56	26.5	70	33.3	48	22.7	3	1.4	25	11.8	9	4.3
D	74	12	16.3	30	40.5	21	28.4	2	2.7	9	12.1	...	...
E	263	77	29.5	39	14.9	39	14.9	5	1.9	56	20.9	47	17.9
F	96	22	22.9	33	34.4	30	31.2	...	...	11	11.5	...	...
G	138	28	20.3	53	38.3	34	24.8	4	2.9	15	10.8	4	2.9
H	105	21	20.0	41	39.0	24	22.8	3	2.9	14	13.4	2	1.9
I	210	41	19.5	64	30.5	44	20.9	14	6.6	37	17.7	10	4.8
J	283	93	32.8	50	17.6	58	20.5	7	2.5	57	20.2	18	6.4
K	400	119	29.8	78	19.5	65	16.3	9	2.3	77	19.1	52	13.0
L	130	43	33.2	36	27.7	22	16.9	2	1.5	18	13.8	9	6.9
P	124	33	25.6	43	34.7	36	30.1	2	1.6	10	8.0	...	...
Q	120	39	32.5	28	23.3	29	24.2	8	6.7	9	7.5	7	5.8
Total	2,456	650	26.5	663	27.2	532	21.6	66	2.6	372	15.1	173	7.0

* Total number of contacts in which the children overtly expressed one or more of the six behavior traits selected for study.

with the children in the group. The fourteen children were grouped into three classes on the basis of the frequency with which their records showed *resistance, aggressiveness,* and *combativeness* when compared with the number of times their contacts showed *resourcefulness* and *initiation of activity*. The records of the first group, E, K, and J, compared favorably in the frequency with which they showed *resourcefulness* in their contacts and in the number of times they *initiated activity*. The records of these three children infrequently showed *resistance, aggressiveness,* and *combativeness* when compared with the records of others. The records of the second group of children, including D, H, G, P, F, and Q, showed contacts in which their behavior was frequently observed as *resistant, aggressive,* and *combative*; and relatively infrequently did these children demonstrate traits that were classified as *resourcefulness* and *initiation of activity*. The members of the third group, including A, B, C, I, and L, ranked in different positions when their records were compared as to the number of times the individual's behavior was classified as *resistance, aggressiveness, combativeness, resourcefulness,* and *initiation of activity*, and also when compared with the records of the children placed in the other two groups.

When the records of the contacts made by thirteen children were compiled, together with the number of times the individual's contacts showed one or more of the six behavior traits, the results showed that the children made more contacts of the type selected for this study at the time their own mothers were assistants than when other mothers were present (see Tables XIII and XIV). Furthermore, the children's records showed a larger incidence of resourcefulness at the time their own mothers were present. At the time other mothers were present they exhibited *co-operation, resistance, aggressiveness, initiation of activity,* and *combativeness* more frequently than when their own mothers were assistants.

The results concerning the child's behavior in the presence of his own mother and of other mothers indicate that (1) no child exhibited the six types of behavior with the same frequency in the two situations; (2) individual differences were shown in the number of times each of the six behavior traits was observed in

TABLE XIII

THE FREQUENCY WITH WHICH THE CHILDREN'S CONTACTS SHOWED THE SIX CLASSES OF BEHAVIOR AT THE TIME THEIR OWN MOTHERS WERE PRESENT

Child	Total Number of Contacts	Co-operation		Resistance		Aggressiveness		Combativeness		Initiation of Activity		Resourcefulness	
		Number	Per Cent	Number	Per Cent	Number	Per Cent	Number	Per Cent	Number	Per Cent	Number	Per Cent
A	71	17	24.0	16	22.6	20	28.2	3	4.2	11	15.4	4	5.6
B* ..	:	:	...	:	...	:	...			:	...	:	...
C	99	26	26.0	34	34.0	29	30.0	2	2.0	6	6.0	2	2.0
D	35	6	17.1	11	31.3	15	42.6	1	3.0	2	6.0	:	...
E	157	40	24.9	18	11.6	12	7.7	3	2.0	47	30.1	37	23.6
F	45	11	24.5	19	42.2	10	22.2		...	5	11.1	:	...
G	70	18	25.7	29	41.4	14	20.0		...	8	11.4	1	1.4
H	66	16	24.0	34	51.0	12	10.0	2	3.0	2	3.0	:	...
I	110	22	20.0	28	25.4	26	23.6	4	3.6	23	20.9	7	6.3
J	143	43	30.0	21	14.6	32	22.4	6	4.2	31	21.6	10	7.0
K	225	62	27.5	63	28.0	39	17.3	4	1.7	21	9.3	36	16.0
L	68	24	35.3	22	32.3	8	12.0	1	1.4	9	13.2	4	5.7
P	64	13	20.2	30	47.0	14	22.0	2	3.1	5	7.6	:	...
Q	76	25	32.9	12	15.8	23	30.2	5	6.5	6	7.8	5	6.5
Total .	1,229	323	26.3	337	27.4	254	20.6	33	2.6	176	14.3	106	8.6

* B's mother did not serve as assistant in the Nursery School.

TABLE XIV

The Frequency with Which the Children's Contacts Showed the Six Classes of Behavior at the Time Other Mothers Were Present

Child	Total Number of Contacts	Co-operation		Resistance		Aggressiveness		Combativeness		Initiation of Activity		Resourcefulness	
		Number	Per Cent	Number	Per Cent	Number	Per Cent	Number	Per Cent	Number	Per Cent	Number	Per Cent
A....	77	13	16.9	30	38.9	20	25.9	1	1.4	6	7.7	7	9.1
B*....	...	:	...	:	...	:	...	:	...	:	...	:	...
C....	112	30	26.7	36	32.2	19	16.9	1	0.9	19	16.9	7	6.2
D....	39	6	15.3	19	48.7	6	15.3	1	2.5	7	18.0	:	...
E....	106	37	34.9	21	19.8	27	25.4	2	1.9	9	8.5	10	9.4
F....	51	11	21.7	14	27.6	20	39.4	:	...	6	11.3	:	...
G....	68	10	14.7	24	35.3	20	29.4	4	6.0	7	10.2	3	4.4
H....	39	5	12.8	7	18.0	12	30.7	1	2.5	12	30.7	2	5.0
I....	100	19	19.0	36	36.0	18	18.0	10	10.0	14	14.0	3	3.0
J....	140	50	35.7	29	20.7	26	18.5	1	0.7	26	18.5	8	5.7
K....	175	57	32.6	15	8.5	26	14.8	5	2.5	56	32.1	16	9.2
L....	62	19	30.5	14	22.6	14	22.6	1	1.6	9	14.5	5	8.2
P....	60	20	33.4	13	21.7	22	36.6	:	...	5	8.3	:	...
Q....	44	14	31.9	16	36.4	6	13.6	3	6.8	3	6.8	2	4.5
Total .	1,073	291	26.7	274	25.3	236	22.3	30	2.8	179	16.7	63	5.9

* B's mother did not serve as assistant in the Nursery School.

the two situations; (3) G failed to show *combativeness* at the time her own mother was assistant, but revealed this trait in her contacts when other mothers were present; P's record failed to show this trait at the time other mothers were present, but exhibited the trait in her contacts when her own mother was assistant; H's record showed that he had a preference for *resourcefulness* when mothers other than his own were present; (4) *co-operation, resistance, aggressiveness,* and *initiation of activity* were exhibited by the individual children both when their own mother and when other mothers were present; (5) the members of the group more frequently exhibited *resourcefulness* in their contacts at the time their own mothers were assistants than when other mothers were present; *co-operation, resistance, aggressiveness,* and *initiation of activity* were each observed more frequently at the time mothers other than the child's own mother were serving as assistants; (6) three children, D, F, and P, were not observed showing *resourcefulness* in their contacts, and F failed to show *combativeness* at the time records were made of their contacts in the Nursery School. However, the foregoing trends are not conclusive.

The experimenter recognized certain factors in the children's experiences at home which apparently influenced the individuals in their contacts with other children. One factor which seemed to enter into the training of the children of this group was the emphasis the mothers placed upon *co-operation* as a desirable trait. In H, F, D, and P's home experiences, co-operation was insisted upon to the extent that the child's readiness and interest in co-operative activities were ignored by the parents. In other family situations, including those of B, J, K, and E, the children learned the techniques of co-operation by participating with adults and with children in the development of common interests. These experiences in the family group seemed to place co-operation on the plane of an opportunity to the individual, and to represent attempts to develop satisfactory techniques and methods of co-operating. In their contacts in the Nursery School, J, B, K, and E showed more discrimination in the co-operative projects they entered. A, who was accepted in his family for the contribution he was able to make, apparently was not disturbed by the infrequency with which he was included in group play if the group activities did not interest him. Children I, C, and G demonstrated apprehension in situations in which they wanted to co-operate and frequently exhibited unsatisfactory techniques through their various attempts at co-operative play. Apparently their inadequate techniques were the result of over-protective methods chosen by their mothers when directing group activities both at home and in the Nursery School. L co-operated to the extent that she was subservient to dictations from members of the group. L's experiences in her family did not include any group interests which L and her parents developed co-operatively.

F was frequently urged by his mother to demonstrate his ability; however, he was allowed only limited opportunities in his home to exhibit any aggressive tendencies. In the Nursery School, F appeared to recognize the release that came from the relaxation of the restrictions he experienced at home and often seemed to gain satisfaction through various types of aggressive behavior.

The experimenter observed that many of the children seemingly experienced more security at the time their own mothers were assistants in the Nursery School than when other mothers were present. It was then that the child demonstrated more independence in the management of his affairs and seemed to feel more freedom in the development of his interests. However, Mothers II, IV, VI, and IX imposed certain restrictions upon their children's activities because of their prejudices for and against certain types of behavior and their over-protective attitude toward their own children. When these four mothers assisted in the Nursery conform more than they did when other mothers were present in the school.

COMPARISON BETWEEN MOTHERS' RATINGS OF CHILDREN AND THE FREQUENCY OF THE SIX BEHAVIOR TRAITS

Each of the mothers who acted as assistants in the Nursery School was asked by the experimenter to rank her own child with respect to his tendency to *co-operate*, to show *resistance*, to be *aggressive*, to exhibit *combative* behavior, to *initiate activity*, and to be *resourceful*. These mothers were asked to make separate ratings of children in the group other than their own, using as the basis for their ratings of the two groups their individual opinion of the position of each child in relation to the group when ranked according to the frequency with which the individual's behavior could be classified as exhibiting one or more of the six behavior traits. The numbers 1 to 14 (greatest to least) were used in classifying the children in terms of these behavior traits. A copy of the rating sheet is given on the opposite page.

The experimenter tabulated the rankings assigned to each child by his own mother based upon the frequency with which she judged that her child or other children exhibited the six behavior traits. An average ranking was calculated for each child based upon the rankings assigned the individuals by mothers other than their own. The mothers' rankings were based upon the frequency with which they judged each child exhibited the six behavior traits in his contacts with other children. The two rankings assigned the individual children as described above, together with the number of times each of the six forms of behavior was noted in the individual's observation record, were each converted into scores for individual children based upon the standard deviation of all rankings and numbers for each of the six classes of behavior. The resulting scores were charted for each child, using the mean as the base, thus showing the relation of the three scores for each child. These comparisons are presented graphically in Charts IV to XVII, inclusive.

The charts reveal that the various ratings and objective scores diverge in many ways. There was a wide range of difference between scores based upon observational records and ratings by mothers other than the child's own mother. The smallest incidence of difference occurred in connection with *combative* behavior, which showed a range of difference from 7.0 to 0.4 sigma. The greatest range of difference occurred in connection with resourcefulness, from 16.6 to 0.6 sigma. K's record showed the greatest differences for an individual when the two scores were

The names of fourteen Nursery School children are on this list. Will you please rank each according to his position in relation to the group? Using numbers 1 to 14 (greatest to least), grade each child with regard to his possession of the characteristics under consideration. For instance, if Child X attempts to *co-operate* more often than any other of the fourteen children, he should receive 1; while if Child Z makes fewer attempts than any of the other children, he should receive 14.

RATING SHEET OF TENDENCIES

Child	Co-operative-ness	Resistance	Aggressiveness	Combativeness	Initiation of Activity	Resourcefulness
A						
B						
C						
D						
E						
F						
G						
H						
I						
J						
K						
L						
P						
Q						

compared on the basis of the six classes of behavior. The average difference revealed in his ratings was 10.0 sigma. A's record showed the smallest differences in the comparison of the two scores, as shown by the average difference of 2.6 sigma for the ratings assigned A in the six forms of behavior.

The scores arrived at for each child based upon observation records were compared with the ranking assigned the child by his *own* mother with regard to the tendency of each child to exhibit the six forms of behavior when compared with other members of the group. K's record showed the greatest range of difference in the two scores on *co-operation*, with a difference of range of 14.1 sigma, whereas the scores of Q and P disclosed the least range of difference, each having a range of difference in scores of 0.5 sigma. The greatest range of differences between the two ratings, 13.7 sigma, occurred in the frequency with which the children exhibited *resourcefulness*. The most limited range of differences, 3.0 sigma, existed when the mothers rated the frequency of *combativeness* in the behavior of their own children.

In a comparison of the ratings by other mothers and by the children's own mothers, J's record showed a range of difference of 11.1 sigma for *co-operativeness*, and H's record showed a range of difference of 0.2 sigma for the same factor. The greatest differences between the ratings occurred in connection with *co-operation*, and the scores of the two groups of mothers showed least variability in their ratings of *initiation of activity* on the part of the children. E's record showed more variability in the scores assigned him by the two groups of mothers than any other of the children, with an average difference of 6.5 sigma. The mothers' scores differed least when the scores for P were compared, showing an average of 2.8 sigma for the six classes of behavior.

This group of mothers seemed to be influenced in their ratings of their own child and of other children by certain factors; however, the data were inadequate in definitely establishing the influence of these factors.

One factor was the apparent lack of objectivity in ranking the children on the frequency with which their own or other children exhibited the behavior traits chosen here for study. Mothers

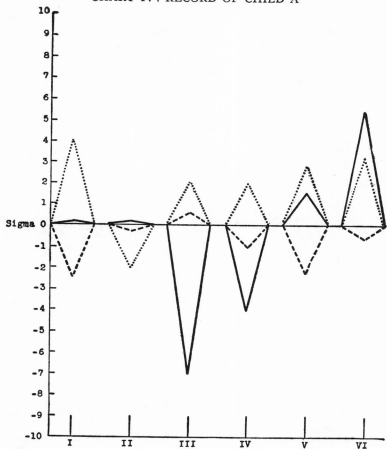

CHART IV: RECORD OF CHILD A

——— Ratings of own mother.

------- Ratings based upon observation records.

...... Ratings of other mothers.

I. Co-operation.
II. Resistance.
III. Aggressiveness.
IV. Combativeness.
V. Initiation of activity.
VI. Resourcefulness.

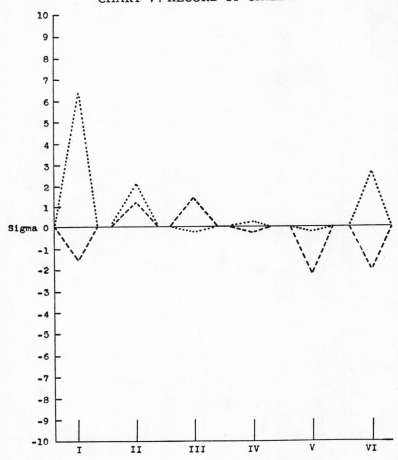

CHART V: RECORD OF CHILD B

——— Ratings of own mother.
------- Ratings based upon observation records.
...... Ratings of other mothers.

I. Co-operation.
II. Resistance.
III. Aggressiveness.
IV. Combativeness.
V. Initiation of activity.
VI. Resourcefulness.

CHART VI: RECORD OF CHILD C

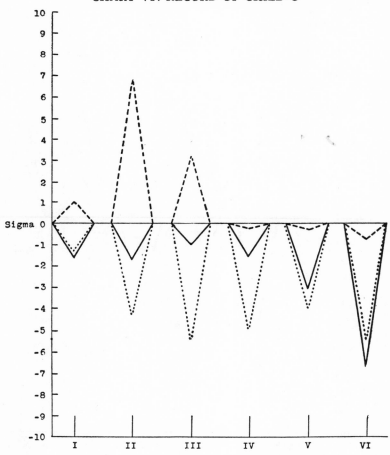

Ratings of own mother.
.... Ratings based upon observation records.
...... Ratings of other mothers.

I. Co-operation.
II. Resistance.
III. Aggressiveness.
IV. Combativeness.
V. Initiation of activity.
VI. Resourcefulness.

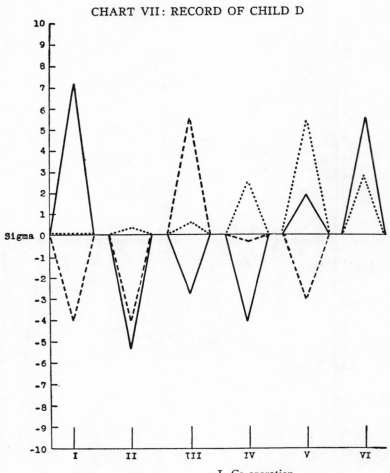

CHART VII: RECORD OF CHILD D

——— Ratings of own mother.
------ Ratings based upon observation
       records.
...... Ratings of other mothers.

I. Co-operation.
II. Resistance.
III. Aggressiveness.
IV. Combativeness.
V. Initiation of activity.
VI. Resourcefulness.

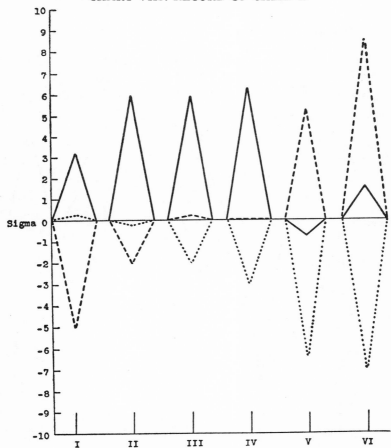

CHART VIII: RECORD OF CHILD E

——— Ratings of own mother.
------ Ratings based upon observation records.
...... Ratings of other mothers.

I. Co-operation.
II. Resistance.
III. Aggressiveness.
IV. Combativeness.
V. Initiation of activity.
VI. Resourcefulness

CHART IX: RECORD OF CHILD F

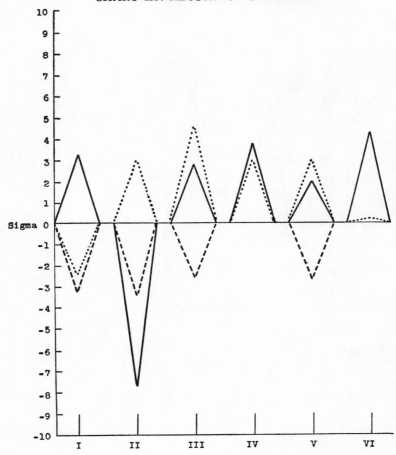

——— Ratings of own mother.	I. Co-operation.
- - - - Ratings based upon observation records.	II. Resistance.
	III. Aggressiveness.
...... Ratings of other mothers.	IV. Combativeness.
	V. Initiation of activity.
	VI. Resourcefulness.

CHART X: RECORD OF CHILD G

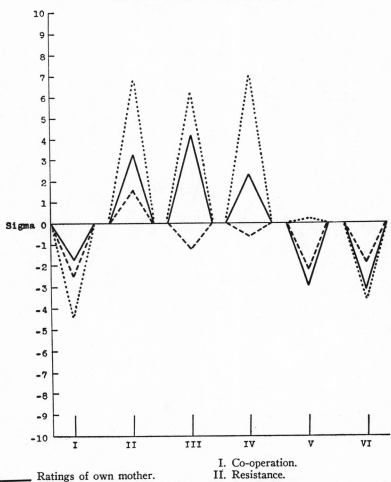

Ratings of own mother.
Ratings based upon observation records.
Ratings of other mothers.

I. Co-operation.
II. Resistance.
III. Aggressiveness.
IV. Combativeness.
V. Initiation of activity.
VI. Resourcefulness.

CHART XI: RECORD OF CHILD H

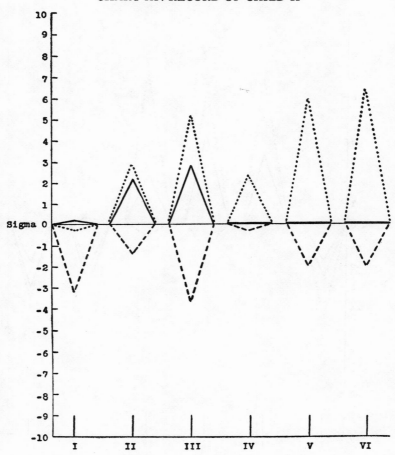

_____ Ratings of own mother.
▪▪▪▪▪▪ Ratings based upon observation
records.
...... Ratings of other mothers.

I. Co-operation.
II. Resistance.
III. Aggressiveness.
IV. Combativeness.
V. Initiation of activity.
VI. Resourcefulness.

CHART XII: RECORD OF CHILD I

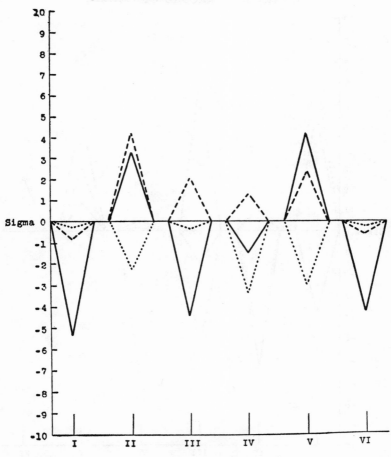

_____ Ratings of own mother.
- - - - - Ratings based upon observation
records.
. . . . . . Ratings of other mothers.

I. Co-operation.
II. Resistance.
III. Aggressiveness.
IV. Combativeness.
V. Initiation of activity.
VI. Resourcefulness.

CHART XIII: RECORD OF CHILD J

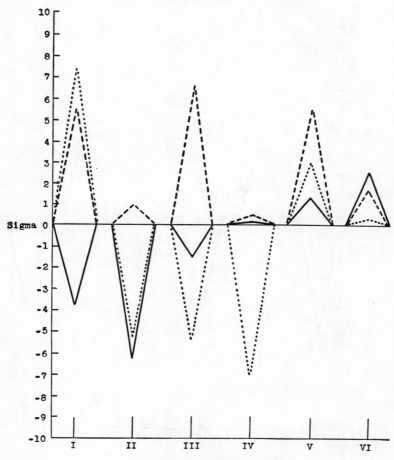

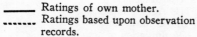

_____ Ratings of own mother.
-------- Ratings based upon observation
        records.
...... Ratings of other mothers.

I. Co-operation.
II. Resistance.
III. Aggressiveness.
IV. Combativeness.
V. Initiation of activity.
VI. Resourcefulness.

CHART XIV: RECORD OF CHILD K

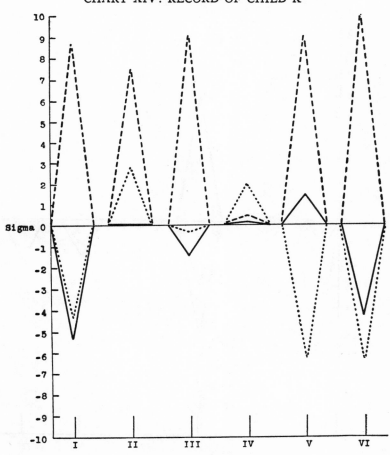

_____ Ratings of own mother.
.... Ratings based upon observation
records.
...... Ratings of other mothers.

I. Co-operation.
II. Resistance.
III. Aggressiveness.
IV. Combativeness.
V. Initiation of activity.
VI. Resourcefulness.

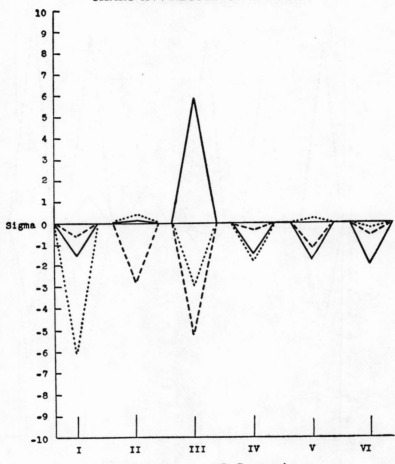

CHART XV: RECORD OF CHILD L

_____ Ratings of own mother.
------- Ratings based upon observation
        records.
...... Ratings of other mothers.

I. Co-operation.
II. Resistance.
III. Aggressiveness.
IV. Combativeness.
V. Initiation of activity.
VI. Resourcefulness.

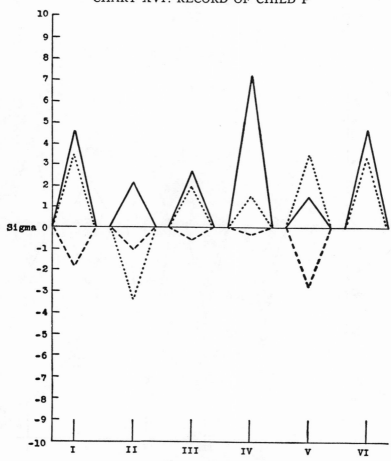

CHART XVI: RECORD OF CHILD P

——— Ratings of own mother.
------- Ratings based upon observation records.
...... Ratings of other mothers.

I. Co-operation.
II. Resistance.
III. Aggressiveness.
IV. Combativeness.
V. Initiation of activity.
VI. Resourcefulness.

CHART XVII: RECORD OF CHILD Q

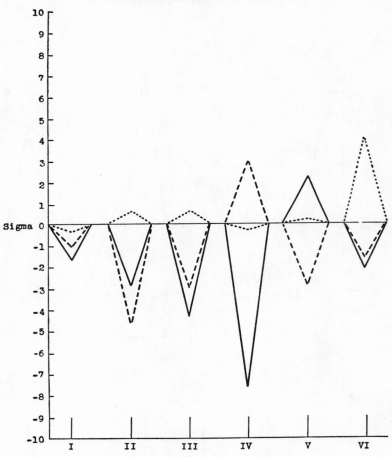

	I. Co-operation.
——— Ratings of own mother.	II. Resistance.
------- Ratings based upon observation	III. Aggressiveness.
records.	IV. Combativeness.
...... Ratings of other mothers.	V. Initiation of activity.
	VI. Resourcefulness.

II, VI, IX, and X apparently had a predisposition for or against certain forms of behavior, including *resistance, combativeness, aggressiveness, resourcefulness,* and *initiation of activity.* Mother II always showed concern in response to any signs of *resistance* or *combativeness,* and her ratings indicate that she was especially aware of such behavior.

Other mothers, including Mothers I, III, V, VI, VII, and XI, appeared not to be much concerned with these forms of behavior, and exhibited less knowledge of the frequency with which *resistant* and *combative* behavior occurred. Mother X apparently approved of the children's protecting themselves and their property rights by physical means, as she frequently coached her child, P, in these methods of protection. Her rankings showed that she was aware of those who settled their differences by such means and of those who made no attempt to do so. Mothers VI and IX each ranked their own children high on the frequency with which they showed *aggressiveness, resourcefulness,* and *initiation of activity.* Each of these mothers frequently expressed a desire for her child to develop these traits.

The age of the children apparently was another factor that caused the mothers to disagree on the ratings. J, K, and E, the oldest members of the group, showed the greatest discrepancies. The younger members of the Nursery School, including D, P, Q, and H, were rated more consistently than were the others by the two groups of mothers.

Seemingly, the intelligence of the child was still another factor which caused disagreements on the mothers' ratings, when compared with the scores based upon observation records. The ratings of K, E, and C, whose records showed intelligence scores classed in the genius and the superior group, showed more frequent disagreements than did the records of any other members of the group. As the children's records classified them in the average intelligence group, as in the case of T, L, P, and Q, the ratings revealed more consistency and the differences in the scores from the two sources became less than was true for the genius and superior groups. A and G were classed in the average group based upon intelligence, and F in the dull average group. In each case the degree of consistency in their rankings varied more in the records of children with an average intelligence than in the records of the child placed in the dull average group.

SUMMARY

1. The fourteen children observed in the Nursery School exhibited the six classes of behavior in the following order of frequency, on the basis of observational records: *resistance, co-operation, aggressiveness, initiation of activity, resourcefulness,* and *combativeness.*

2. There were three children who frequently exhibited *resourcefulness* and *initiation of activity* in their contacts, but who relatively infrequently engaged in behavior classified as *resistance, aggressiveness,* and *combativeness.* A second group, including six children, frequently revealed *resistance, aggressiveness,* and *combativeness* throughout their contacts, and relatively infrequently was their behavior classified as evidence of *initiation of activity* and *resourcefulness.* The remaining six children showed no consistent trend.

3. The children exhibited *resourcefulness* more frequently when their own mothers were assistants than in the presence of other mothers. They exhibited relatively more *co-operation, resistance, aggressiveness, initiation of activity,* and *combativeness* at the time mothers other than their own were present.

4. In a comparison of the z-scores derived from (*a*) the average rating assigned to each child by all the mothers exclusive of his own mother who served in the Nursery School and (*b*) the frequency of contacts secured from the observation records for each of the six behavior traits under consideration, the following differences were noted: (1) the mothers' ratings of *aggressive* behavior were at the widest variance with the observed *aggressiveness* of the children, while their ratings of *combativeness* were in closest agreement (of the six factors studied) with the observed *combativeness* of the children; and (2) the range between z-scores assigned these fourteen children on the basis of observed contacts and the rankings of mothers other than their own was

greatest in the case of *co-operation* and smallest in the case of *combativeness*.

5. A comparison of the scores based upon observation records with the ranking assigned each child by his own mother showed greatest difficulty in estimating the frequency with which the children's activities revealed *resourcefulness*. When their ratings were compared with the children's records, the mothers' records showed that they estimated more accurately the frequency with which their own children exhibited *combativeness* in their contacts with other children than was true of their ratings of any other behavior factor studied.

6. The ratings of the two groups of mothers, including the child's own mother and other mothers, were compared. The greatest differences appeared in the ratings of *co-operation* and the smallest disagreement was shown in the ratings of *initiation of activity*.

Chapter VII
RECORDS OF MOTHERS AND CHILDREN

THIS chapter describes interrelations between the eleven mothers and the fourteen children in the Co-operative Nursery School. It is based upon outstanding characteristics shown by the observation records in (1) the practices employed by the mothers, (2) the activities of the children in which the mothers were participants, and (3) individual differences in the behavior of children as manifested by *co-operation, aggressiveness, combativeness, resourcefulness,* and the frequency with which the child *initiated activities.* Additional information was provided by the opportunities which the experimenter had to make contacts with mothers and children in their homes, and also through longer periods of observation in the Nursery School situations than those afforded the observer when making records.

MOTHER I AND CHILD A

The family consisted of mother, father, A, and a sister two years older than A. A maid was employed who was responsible for the routine housekeeping duties, but who had no part in the care and guidance of the children.

The father, a lawyer, had a well-established clientele. Added financial security was given the family through an inheritance received by both father and mother from their families. The total income, which was not large, was budgeted by the family members and spent after the needs of each member had been considered by the group. The mother served efficiently in the capacity of business manager for the family.

The father was an easy-going, happy person who seemed to think that many of the problems in life, especially those affecting the adjustment of the individual to his environment, were best solved by doing little about them and, at the same time, keeping busy. He was actively interested in two civic organizations, and brought home many interesting details, not only regarding his work, but also about recent developments in his many avocations.

The mother's main interest was the life of her family, which she directed with skill. The details of housekeeping seemed to have little effect upon the serenity with which she viewed life in general as well as the specific problems for adjustment found in her own home. She studied her situation and seemed to evaluate the factors affecting her family, approaching each problem with confidence and at the same time with awareness of its differing value for each member of the family.

Mother I displayed much more interest in the older child, who is a girl, than in A, and manifested great pride in showing off this child's skill in certain feats involving physical co-ordination and mental alertness. As a rule, she viewed A, who was over-grown and blundering, with a passive interest, but at times appeared thoroughly amused at his attempts to make social contacts or to use play equipment, the manipulation of which required muscular co-ordination and mental agility.

Mother I's activities in the Nursery School were characterized by an awareness of important happenings in the school situations, and by a calmness in directing the group and an objective attitude toward the individual child. Mother I showed much skill in absenting herself from situations when the child or the children involved showed interest or progress.

The composure with which Mother I directed the children is shown by the practices she employed. She seldom employed such terms as "Hurry up," or other comments or practices which indicated impatience. If the child was in immediate danger of physical disaster, she used practices which *impeded* his progress, with relatively infrequent use of the practices classified as *warns* and *forces*. In situations in which the child or the children apparently were interested but unskilled, Mother I's record indicates that she used practices classified as *encourages, commends,* and *reassures*.

There is no evidence that Mother I was effusive and indiscriminate in her methods of *commendation* of her child or of the other children in the Nursery School. The situations in which she *expressed her approval* were the ones in which the child or children had shown a willingness to *co-operate*.[1] Apparently, she had an appreciation of the child's or children's sincerity.

Mother I's record shows no discrimination toward the children she contacted during her period of assisting in the school. The children's records show that they were more *successful in carrying out Mother I's instructions* than those of any of the other mothers; yet there is no evidence that there was any overpowering dominance of the children by Mother I. The routine and play activities of the school passed off with relative serenity, as Mother I's record shows no *conflicts*, a fact which was due apparently to her ability to foresee difficulties and to her insight into the progress of undesirable behavior on the part of individuals as the group engaged in co-operative activities.

The records show that A went through the activities of the Nursery School with few crises occurring in his behavior. He was patient with himself and showed confidence in himself, but he lacked the technique of making contacts which were satisfactory to him and to the children with whom he associated in the school. His patience toward himself and toward others seemed to reflect the attitude of his family members.

A was co-operative in carrying out instructions given him by adults and seemed pleased to have them give him specific and definite directions. This is quite plausible in the light of the practices which Mother I used with A, which, in all instances, were direct and definite.

A attempted to use all play and routine equipment, but frequently his progress was slow, although he never became discouraged to the point of deserting his pursuit. He often watched with much interest the manipulation of play and routine equipment by other children, and when they had cast it aside he would begin to experiment. He was frequently confronted by the alertness and ease with which other children manipulated equipment, but his overt behavior gave no evidence of antagonism toward other children who succeeded better than he in carrying out various activi-

---

[1] Mother I's records show no emphasis upon any one situation except the *toileting* situation, which fact may be partially explained in that Mother I was the first assistant in the Nursery School.

ties. His lack of skill and technique seemed to be a barrier to his development of co-operative contacts with children of his age and with older children.

A seemed to hold the position of a "buffer" in the group. Very seldom was he sufficiently upset to cry, yet he demonstrated ability to protect himself and his property by all the methods usually employed by children when interfered with by older children.

The mothers' practices directed toward A were more frequently classified as *directs, seeks information,* and *encourages* than as any other practices. The practices classified as *urges, impedes,* and *forces* were used relatively infrequently when A's record was compared with that of other children. The mothers apparently learned early in their assistantship at the Nursery School that A was thwarted in his progress by any demonstration of tenseness or exasperation at his efforts.

CHILD B AND HIS PARENTS

B's mother did not act as assistant in the Nursery School; however, it is interesting to supplement the picture of B, as shown in his activities at school, with some of the facts presented by his home situation which seem pertinent in the development of his personality.

B's father was a professional man. The other members of B's family were an older brother and sister who gave him much attention when out of school, including him as a partner in many of their play activities. The physical care of B and his training in habit formation were left entirely to the maid. B's father and mother were interested in the child and spent much of their time with him when they were at home; but they were both impressed with the importance of an objective parental contact, and acted in accordance with this theory. They had much confidence in B's ability to take care of himself; and B showed an unlimited amount of sureness as he manipulated toys and play equipment. He apparently had no fear, and was an adept at climbing, running, and in the use of any toys or play equipment requiring skill in motor co-ordination.

B's brother and sister showed pride in his achievements and encouraged him to follow them in their play activities, at the same time watching him and frequently assisting him in the use of play equipment and helping him to develop skill and to succeed in developing his interests. The emergencies in which B was involved in the Nursery School were usually due to his lack of judgment in estimating either his strength or his ability to perform certain activities which he had either initiated himself or had observed some older child carry through.

B, according to his records, showed the most frequent resistance in the *toileting* situations, in *emergency* situations, and in situations where his *clothes were exchanged* or *wraps removed*. The *toileting* situation may be partially accounted for by the handling he received from the maid, who was responsible for the development of his physical habits. B's clothes were poorly chosen without any thought of his problem to manipulate them himself, and they were usually pinned in such a manner that he needed assistance in unfastening them.

B was directed relatively frequently by the mothers, as is shown by his record when compared with that of other children. He was one of the youngest members of the group, and the mothers gave more attention to his needs than to those of any other child. They were most solicitous toward B and toward his physical needs, and their apprehension in the play situations may be judged by the frequency with which they attempted to *divert B's attention* to activities they judged were suitable.

The mothers used the practice classified as *impedes* more frequently with B and C than with any other children of the group. B's record shows the situations in which his progress was *impeded* and indicates that they occurred in the *play* situations, while he was *reassured, commended,* and *urged* in the routine situations to the exclusion of any of these practices in the *play* situations. *Explanations were offered* B relatively infrequently, and in each *play* situation the explanations seemed to be part of the mother's technique in convincing B that the activity he was engaged in was undesirable. In the routine situations the explanations seemed to be used as one means of *urging* B to initiate a routine. B was guided by those practices classified as *directs* with approximately the same frequency as other children of the same age level; however, this practice was used most frequently in the routine situations.

MOTHER II AND CHILD G

G was the only child in his family. The profession which the father temporarily followed was one which was not in line with his chosen vocation. The mother, before the child was born, had been actively engaged in professional life; but after that time she accepted only part-time positions in her specialized field. The rearing of the child was looked upon by the mother as a business proposition into which she merged all her abilities and interests. The father, a jovial person, accepted the role of an amused spectator as he watched the mother play her earnest and intense part in the drama of rearing the child. The home, with the assistance of a full-time maid, was kept in the best condition at all times. The responsibility for the child was assumed in its entirety by the mother. She was easily upset by any changes that had to be made in the family routine, and was tense if any new and varied problems appeared on the horizon of any member of the family. She apparently feared the new and untried for herself, but even more for her child, over whom she watched with an eagle eye.

When Mother II acted as assistant in the Nursery School, her records show the use of fewer words and fewer practices than those of any other mother in the group, and the children in turn talked to her less frequently than to any other mother, as shown by the infrequent verbal contacts which she made.

Mother II's records reveal that she gave the children painstaking attention, never allowing an activity to go unnoticed. The observer noted in her records comments of the following type describing Mother II's behavior: "Mother II watches closely the activities of . . . ," "Mother II moves so that she can see the activities of . . . ," etc. The children, during the time that Mother II acted as assistant, showed very little variation in the types of play activities engaged in. If the children began to use a new piece of equipment which she had not observed them using, Mother II directed them into the more frequent use of familiar activities and permitted fewer of the exploratory methods of using routine and play equipment. In getting children to change plans and methods, she did not suggest possible activities from which the children could make a choice, but directed them to begin a familiar type of activity. Mother II was apparently aware of her fear of the untried and was unable to assume a relaxed attitude when the children were using equipment which required physical skill and alertness. She *urged* the children to initiate routine activities and stressed carrying through and completing routines in perfect fashion. Mother II was apparently shy in ordinary contacts with children, a characteristic which completely vanished as soon as she took part in a routine activity or any activity in which she enacted the role of instructor. She was hesitant, however, about entering into the *free-play* activities unless she detected a lack of skill in the use of play equipment or inadequate techniques in group play. She used the practice described as *discourages* once during the observation period, and it seemed that she frequently studied the situations to detect any activity for which she felt the child or children could be *commended, encouraged,* and *reassured.* She appeared nervous if she made a request of a child, and frequently responded to a verbal request by answering herself; however, she never *overlooked* any duty left unfinished or any routine activity in which the child attempted to change the order or methods of solution.

There were children in the group for whom Mother II showed a preference. These were the youngest members, and a child whom she considered was being neglected by his mother and for whom she occasionally expressed sympathy. This child contacted Mother II more frequently than any other member of the group, even more often than her own child. These preferences were shown by the mother's solicitous attitude in helping them through routines and in her determination to have their play activities successful and free from crises. The older children and the most aggressive individuals within the group, including the most intelligent, were given less consideration in time and order of routine and less guidance in the selection and use of play equipment. She watched over this latter group, but often turned away and left the locality if approached by a member of the group. The children in turn withdrew from her presence after completing the activity in which she had participated.

She frequently approached the children to inquire about their physical comfort and needs, often adjusting a child's clothing without the child's knowledge. In the *toileting* situations Mother II used many methods of teaching the child the routine activities and frequently *encouraged* the child to take care of his clothing and of the equipment. In the *mid-morning lunch* and *rest* situations, Mother II seemed to be less anxious, and the children's records reveal more frequent success. In the *emergency* situations and situations in which *conflicts* occurred, Mother II's practices were very concise and direct, and she used methods of *impeding* if she judged that the child's activities might lead into danger, and used the same method in directing a child whom she seemed to judge had the advantage in a *conflict*.

In the routine situations and in one non-routine situation, the *instructional*, Mother II was more relaxed than in the other three non-routine situations. In routine and *instructional* periods, Mother II directed the children in the details of their activities, using every opportunity to teach the individual child by frequently inserting a teaching situation into a routine one, taking as her object lesson something in which she apparently considered the child might find some interest. She never waited for a request for help, but gave it before the child was aware of any need for assistance.

G, a well-developed, slightly awkward child, showed much interest in other children and in play activities and materials, but her techniques for making social contacts and using play materials were poor.

G was the most unsuccessful child in the group in making contacts with strange children or in finding uses for play equipment other than those familiar to her. For example, she had to be urged and coaxed by the teacher in the Nursery School before she could be persuaded to use any climbing equipment, and then only when the teacher stood near and told her exactly how to climb. As soon as the teacher withdrew her verbal assistance, G would retreat to the ground. She was apparently influenced in her interests and activities by words of *encouragement*, a gesture or nod from the adult signifying the adult's approval was very often of much assistance to her. This need for encouragement probably was the result of treatment G received at home, as Mother II apparently was on guard and noted each type of behavior exhibited by G which she could use for a basis of encouragement. G frequently appeared to be sizing up the adult and trying to make her decision according to the wishes of the adult.

The children of the group paid very little attention to G's activities, as she was usually content to repeat activities and to carry through play interests which the individuals and the group had already exhausted. Frequently, when she became interested in a co-operative play activity, she suddenly became too aggressive for her playmate, with the result that the latter either retaliated by engaging in a *conflict* or else quietly retired to a more agreeable situation.

Apparently the mothers considered the importance of routine activities in G's development, as they guided G through routines with order and precision after having observed, at intervals, Mother II's guidance in the Nursery School group and heard her discussion in group conferences. The mothers frequently *reassured, encouraged,* and *commended* G for attempts which passed unnoticed as a part of other children's activities, and methods of *impeding* her progress were infrequently used. G was neither *forced* into any activity nor *warned* of any danger during the observation periods. In contrast to the constant guidance and protection given G in all her activities by her own mother was the attitude of other mothers when acting as assistants. They showed confidence in G's ability to take care of herself and to work out her own interests by the practices they chose and by the freedom they allowed her in expressing her individuality in the use of play equipment and in making contacts with other children.

MOTHER III AND CHILD K

K was the only child in the family at the time this study was made. His father was temporarily out of his chosen profession and employed in a less technical profession. This position was very distasteful to him, yet he expressed much gratitude for having steady work. He was actively interested in K, and they spent much time together, inventing and playing games. K's mother was engaged in part-time work when she could secure it. When she was employed, a maid was engaged to do the housework and assume some of the care of K. The remainder of the time each member of the family, including K, was given definite tasks and shared in the housekeeping.

Mother III, who was happy and jovial, was always very agreeable with the children. She often manifested interest in the children by asking questions about their problems, or by commenting upon changes she had observed in their behavior. The children approached Mother III with ease, and she laughed and talked with them as they participated in routine and non-routine situations. She showed a remarkable sense of humor in these situations, and often unwittingly made a child who had shown much restraint in the presence of other assistant mothers appear at ease with her.

She gave the children many opportunities to express their needs in relation to routine and, with the exception of the children in the youngest group, accepted their decisions. The decisions of the younger members of the group were frequently overlooked, and the children were taken into the routine.

K made a greater number of contacts with other children in the group than did any other child in the school. He apparently considered L a satellite and dictated her activities with much skill, offering suggestions that were favorably regarded by her. K paid little attention to the younger members of the group except as they proved their skill in developing *his* interests. He gave evidence of a wide range of interests and was able to follow them through in detail with results that showed much originality. The companion he apparently enjoyed most was E, who also showed much resourcefulness and imagination as he developed his interests through play and the use of the school materials and equipment.

K would not allow the assistant mother to overlook or forget him, and devised various methods of *attracting the attention of adults to himself and to his activities.* A certain group of mothers, including Mothers II, IV, and IX, showed displeasure at his attempts to secure their undivided attention. Since he showed a limited need for *reassurance,* they *discouraged* him relatively frequently as compared with the records of other children, and seldom offered any word of praise or *commendation* for the results he obtained. K was rated the highest in intelligence of any member of the group, and the methods he devised for attracting the attention of adults were interesting even to those prejudiced against him.

Consistency is shown in the choice of practices made by the mothers as they guided J, E, and K, who were members of the oldest group and were near the same chronological age. They were guided by the practice, *directs,* and by *urges* and *encourages* less frequently than members of the younger groups. K's record shows more frequent use of the practices, *offers explanation* and *reassures,* and he in turn *sought information* more frequently than any other member of this group of three children. He was directed less frequently by practices classified as *diverts attention, impedes,* and *overlooks* than was J or E.

MOTHER IV AND CHILD C

Mother IV's family consisted of C and the father. The mother's interests were dominated by social affairs; however, she showed an over-active and wholehearted interest in her family, particularly in C. The father's activities seemed to be largely dictated by the mother, and at the time this study was made the family was experiencing much insecurity, apparently as a result of financial and social adjustments that were necessary at the time. Mother IV seemed to center her interests and attention upon C because of the security she experienced through her contacts with the child.

Mother IV assumed very little responsibility in the Nursery School when she served as assistant. Most of her time was spent in lavishing attention upon her own child, C. She *warned, commended,* and *reassured* C to the exclusion of the other children. She *sought information* from C twenty times, from other children in the group, four times; and in other types of practices she directed the greatest number of her practices toward C, except those used to *urge, impede,* and *discourage* the progress of other children. Mother IV used words of *endearment* more frequently than any other mother in the group, all of which were directed to C. Her records show more frequent use of *polite phrases* with all of the children than do the records of any other mother in the group.

Mother IV, as she directed the children in the group, manifested little interest in individual children other than her own. She showed a partiality for children whom she knew outside of school, including G, H, and I, and exhibited indifference toward, and frequently seemed to resent, the suggestions and activities of the older members of the group, including J, E, and K. She directed the children through all activities upon the basis of an apparently predetermined plan all her own, and she seldom digressed from this plan even at the request of a child or a group of children.

Mother IV directed the children more frequently in the *toileting* situation than in any other routine situation. She demonstrated no interest in the *instructional* situations, and entered into the *free-play* situations only when younger members of the group exhibited a difficulty in the use of play equipment, or when the children, G, H, and I, were involved in the activity, and likewise when her own child, C, was a participant.

The children carried out Mother IV's suggestions successfully, never manifesting any disapproval of the requests she made or showing any resistance to the practices used and carrying them out with little assistance.

The apparent result of Mother IV's concentration upon C was the child's dependence and her demand for attention, especially from adults. C never appeared to be intensely interested in any activity, and used inglorious methods of attracting the attention of adults.

C gave evidence of nervousness in the Nursery School by biting her nails, picking her nose, and exhibiting an unusual amount of restless behavior. Her daily reports from home showed that she had difficulty in going to sleep and that she screamed and talked when asleep. The mother was requested to give less time to C at home and to relieve herself of all routine responsibilities as far as it was possible to delegate such duties to a maid. This method of treatment resulted in less frequent nervous behavior on the part of the child and a more concentrated interest in other children's interests and activities. C made more contacts with members of the group than did any other child in the two-year-old group. In all her activities, as she flitted from one play interest to another and from adults to children, she apparently tried to focus attention upon herself and her activities.

The techniques employed by C were not acceptable to other children. She had no ideas to offer, showed no independence or originality in the use of play equipment, and would not follow the leadership of any child. She was, therefore, not readily accepted as a member of any group.

She apparently expected a great amount of attention from each mother who served as assistant, and her records show that a greater number of practices were directed toward C than toward any other child. She was directed less frequently than any other of the children in the two-year-old group by those practices classified as *directs*. She was *commended, encouraged,* and *reassured* frequently when compared with other children in the same age group. She was *urged, impeded, discouraged,* and *warned* less frequently; however, her records show that she was *overlooked* more frequently than was any other child in the group by the mothers who acted as assistants in the Nursery School.

MOTHER V AND CHILD D

At the time this study was made, Mother V's family consisted of her husband and one child, D. Mother V was interested in many phases of social and historical development. The father, who was interested in a specialized field of his profession, had been successful in securing recognition for research he had completed. There were ease and freedom in this household, as the details of living were never emphasized and seemed to be relatively unimportant to both father and mother. One full-time maid was employed for the necessary housekeeping duties; at times, however, she assisted in the care of D and helped her with routine problems.

Mother V talked very little to either children or adults, unless first approached by them. Then she conversed with ease, apparently appreciating the fact that advances had been made. Mother V approached the problems of the Nursery School with an objective attitude, becoming little exercised over any situation that arose, whether pertaining to the welfare of her own child or to that of other children in the group, except the situations in which D, in her behavior, showed dependence.

Mother V, herself the youngest member of a large family, was inexperienced in the care of children, as she had had no professional or semi-professional interest in them before her own child was born. She showed much interest in the development of D as a personality, but at times became very irritated when the child cried or failed to use acceptable social techniques, and applied methods that retarded the progress of the child's activities. Mother V's record shows the greatest frequency in the use of the practice described as *impedes*. However, she used this and similar practices more readily with her own child than with other children in the group. She used practices that are classified as *discourages* with her own child, reserving the practices designated as *directs, seeks information, offers explanation,* and similar methods of *encouragement* for other children. The children approached Mother V when they were aware of a need or had something concrete to point out as the result of their activities.

Mother V[2] approached the children frequently on the problems

---

[2] Mother V did not assist in the *rest* situation, as D was having difficulty at the time in relaxing and resting. The experimenter took responsibility for the *rest* period at this time in order to use consistent methods with D.

of *toileting*, reminding them of their responsibility in attending to their physical needs at the appropriate time. She conducted the *instructional* periods with interest, teaching the children as a group, and never singling out any one child for instruction. During the *free-play* periods, Mother V was always alert to the activities of the children and responded to any request made by them when they initiated a contact. In the *emergency* and *conflict* situations, Mother V was always objective in her attitude and little disturbed by the happenings. She ordinarily assumed the role of an interested spectator in *conflicts*, but entered into the situation at the appeal of one of the children or to protect a child from injury or further insult.

D was the youngest member of the group and had played with very few children before she came to the Nursery School. She showed much dependence upon her mother in the changed environment, but never relied upon any other adult. She played alone a greater part of the time, entering into activities with B, who was near her age, more frequently than with any other child.

The behavior D demonstrated in her contacts was approximately equal in the frequency with which it was classified as *co-operation* and *resistance*. D employed *combative* methods with relative infrequency, but she used clever techniques in securing the desired toy or play equipment from another child. She was independent in the activities in which she participated, and was irritated by her inability to use play equipment with the skill possessed by older members of the group. D sometimes watched other children use toys and equipment, waiting patiently for them to finish. After a period of concentrated watching, she would employ the same methods they had used, frequently achieving success beyond her years in handling equipment.

The most interesting characteristics of the practices used by the mothers in directing D were the responsibility they apparently gave D for expressing her needs and their willingness to let her be independent in finding her interests and in the development of her play activities. D was slow in her movements and decisions, and there was some evidence in the mothers' records that they were impatient with D, more frequently using practices classified as *urges* than with any other child in the group. The mothers apparently observed no behavior which they judged *expressed insecurity* in D, as they *encouraged* and *commended* D relatively infrequently, and D was not *reassured* during the periods of observation.

MOTHER VI AND CHILD F

The family of Mother VI included F, a younger boy, and the father. The mother seemed to be an extreme extrovert, reacting openly and with apparent honesty to situations as they arose in her life. Her interests were centered in her family life, from which radiated a wide circle of social contacts which she considered necessary for the advancement of her husband and for her own happiness.

The father seemed to be an extreme introvert who contributed very little except financial security to the life of the family. Decisions relating to the family were reached after mother and father had talked over the situation, but it was the mother who made the decisions. The father seemed to consider passive acquiescence the wisest procedure. One full-time maid was employed, whose principal responsibility was the care of the house. A schedule of duties was planned by the mother and effectively executed by the maid, a congenial person who enjoyed her contacts with the children.

Mother VI laughed and talked freely with the children. They, in turn, expressed more interest in her than in any other mother who assisted, and frequently made requests of her. She offered to show them how to dance, how to march, and often entertained the entire group. She accepted the responsibility of caring for the younger members of the group with very little interest; while never showing irritation at their lack of independence, she gave no signs of interest in their progress. The children accepted for the time being the activities to which Mother VI directed them, but frequently *failed in carrying out her requests*; and she, in turn, *overlooked* many of the requests she had made and many of the problems she had pointed out to the children. Mother VI manifested no decided preference for any child within the group, although she showed a keener appreciation of K, J, and E and of their activities than of any other of the children. Mother VI emphasized the importance of the development of acceptable *toileting* habits and frequently reminded the children of their responsibility in going to the toilet at the right time and in developing independence and self-reliance in the activities connected with the *toileting* situation.[3]

Mother VI was very careful to see that a child's clothing was properly arranged for its comfort and convenience. She frequently adjusted the children's scarfs, gloves, collars, and openings in their outside clothing to add to their comfort.

Other routine problems were solved easily and quickly. The children were always interested during the period in which Mother VI read to them or directed them in music and games or in the use of clay in modeling. She allowed her alertness and interest in teaching the children to carry over into the *free-play* period by injecting herself into their activities, continuing to point out and to explain objects and activities which she considered interesting from their point of view.

Mother VI endeavored to dominate F, allowing him little latitude in making plans or decisions for himself. Ordinarily he acquiesced to his mother's rulings at home. However, he occasionally passed through periods of rebellion, openly resenting her practices and destroying toys and play equipment in defiance of the tyranny imposed upon him. F was a responsive child, a fact which his mother apparently doubted. He accepted responsibility readily, as was shown by his habit of making known to the experimenter his physical needs and interests in play activities. He had shown *resistance* to the *toileting* activities at home, but he readily adjusted himself to the *toileting* situation at the Nursery School, and no necessity arose to remind him of his responsibilities.

F's record shows relatively infrequent contacts with children

---

[3] Mother VI had experienced much difficulty with F in the development of habits of elimination. How much these difficulties affected Mother VI's practices in the Nursery School is not determined by the nature of the data gathered in this study.

in the Nursery School. He was content to watch the children use toys or play equipment and often laughed at the results obtained; but he made no attempt to participate unless solicited, and his interest in the activity or apparatus disappeared when his interest in the participants was exhausted. F, when invited to join groups, usually served as a member who carried out an uninteresting detail, and was not asked to contribute ideas or to suggest methods of solving a problem. He always agreed to enter the activity and co-operated as he was told.

F was accepted by the assistant mothers as a child to be conducted through routine activities and to be safeguarded against any injury that he might encounter in his play activities. Outside of these interests, F was guided through the various situations with few attempts at interesting him in differing activities and with few explanations offered by the mothers, although he never received a rebuff from the mothers and the records give no evidence that he was ignored.

F was guided through the Nursery School by practices that differed only in a few instances from those used with other children in the group. F was *warned* more frequently than any other child, apparently because the mothers accepted a sincere responsibility for his welfare and not because F was not cautious in the development of his play interests. The mothers' records show more frequent use of the practice, *commends,* in directing F than for any other child in the group. Apparently the mothers used every occasion to *commend* F for his co-operative attitude in the situations which arose in the Nursery School and for any interest he manifested in play or for any need he expressed in a routine situation.

MOTHER VII AND CHILD L

Mother VII's family consisted of two children, one younger than L, and the husband. The father was temporarily unemployed, but apparently the family was financially secure. Mother VII's interests were never overwhelming in character, and most of the time she assumed a carefree, irresponsible attitude toward her family and their problems. The husband accepted his children as part of life, but manifested very little perceptible interest in their problems or activities.

Mother VII accepted the responsibilities of assistant in the Nursery School in a half-hearted fashion. She used the practice classified as *directs* with the greatest frequency, accompanied by little expenditure of energy or time in giving children *explanations, encouragement,* and *commendation,* practices which she seldom employed. She talked very little to the children except in giving directions in routine situations, and the children responded to Mother VII by answering her questions and making very few requests of her.

The only happenings in the Nursery School that seemed to arouse her interest were accidents that occurred in routine activities that demanded her attention. She was more concerned over the *toileting* situation than over any other, as shown by the practices she used in that situation; and she frequently *warned* the child if he showed any signs of failure to announce his physical needs to her. Mother VII was uninterested in any form of *instruction,* and often relied upon one of the children to entertain the group rather than make any effort herself. She entered into the children's activities during the *free-play* periods only at their instance, and her own child was the one who usually insisted. She allowed *conflicts* to be settled by the children, offering suggestions when one participant was in danger of getting hurt or when she was appealed to for a decision.

The children *failed in carrying out Mother VII's instructions* as frequently as they *succeeded.* The children's records show that they *expressed their interests* and *requested assistance* relatively infrequently. Apparently the children actively co-operated with Mother VII, accepting her guidance, as the records of the children show frequent occurrences of *accepting assistance* passively, in contrast with infrequent occurrences of *doing the task independently.*

L was very conscious of her mother's presence in the Nursery School situations, and frequently called the mother's attention to her activities, apparently seeking *commendation* and approval from her mother.[4] Mother VII occasionally appeared embarrassed at the child's attempts to secure her notice, frequently *overlooking* them or pretending to be occupied.

L was a quiet, unobtrusive child in her contacts with other children, following the leadership of K to the exclusion of all other children. She obeyed his dictates gladly, defended him against any encroachment, and carefully carried out his plans. L was less resourceful than J, E, and K, with whom she most often developed her play interests. She frequently became involved in *conflicts*, and usually withdrew unless the conflict involved K or unless her mother was present. If K was the aggressor or the defendant, she supported him rather passively, and if her mother was in the school, she appealed to her immediately for aid.

No mother singled L out from the group and demonstrated any interest in her activities. They neither guided L in her behavior nor demonstrated any attempts to change her interests or activities.

MOTHER VIII AND CHILDREN E AND J

Mother VIII was a quiet, affable person apparently interested only in the affairs of her family and in the professional success of her husband. The family consisted of a boy and a girl in the Nursery School, an older daughter, and the mother and father. The husband exhibited no active interest in any of the children except the boy, E, who he wished would follow in his profession. Mother VIII exhibited greater interest in the older daughter and showed more interest in this daughter's achievements than in J's.

The home was comfortably arranged, and apparently the family was financially secure. Two maids were employed in the home, one for housekeeping responsibilities, and the other being entirely responsible for the training and care of E and J.

Mother VIII talked freely with the children as she directed them in their routine activities, frequently *commending* them, usually

[4] There was some evidence that L was jealous of the younger child in the family. At home she watched her mother very closely, appearing unhappy and depressed when the mother gave the baby any care. At school, L demanded attention from her mother and often appeared embarrassed as she directed her mother's attention to something which was a mere excuse for attracting notice.

by *phrases not related to the task*. She *encouraged* them frequently and used *impeding* practices infrequently. She *warned* the children by calling attention to methods of avoiding danger, yet she showed no undue alarm at accidents in the Nursery School. She apparently was very sympathetic with any child who cried or who showed any signs of an emotional disturbance, and immediately *reassured* him, offering *encouragement* and less frequently attempting to *divert the child's attention elsewhere*. She was very attentive to the younger members of the group, frequently requesting a child to perform a task and *commending* him before the child had responded. Any child who made a request of Mother VIII received her undivided attention until the child's interest was satisfactorily directed, or he had received the information asked for.

Mother VIII spent much of her time in the *toileting* situation, making many more contacts with the children in this situation than in any other. She apparently guided the children through other routine and play situations with ease and efficiency, but exhibited no interest in *instructing* the children in any situation, including the one in which the children were usually given more formal instruction. She entered into the *free-play* situations at the request of the children, who frequently sought her guidance in solving their problems of play.

The children responded verbally to Mother VIII with relative infrequency, but they carried out successfully the instructions she offered. The children *accepted Mother VIII's assistance passively* and *asked for assistance* infrequently, for apparently she was aware of their needs and interests before they made requests or showed any confusion in their behavior. The children seemed to feel free, when given an opportunity, to *give information* and to *offer explanations*. They *cried* with relatively high frequency at the time Mother VIII was observed. This fact may be partially explained by the coincidence that Mother VIII's observation came first on the schedule. Some of the *crying* observed, therefore, may be attributed to the children's experiences in adaptation to the Nursery School as they exhibited other behavior, showing they were making satisfactory adjustments and were not unduly disturbed.

Mother VIII was excessively attentive to J at times and attempted to help her make acceptable social contacts with members of the group. She showed tenseness in her contacts with J, occasionally giving evidence of embarrassment. She would frequently lavish attention upon J, followed by withdrawal and an objective treatment of the child and her activities amounting to virtual indifference. She paid very little attention to E, and yet showed much pride in his interests and activities. Mother VIII apparently guided E with much less effort, and used more consistency in her treatment of him than of J.

E was active in the Nursery School and exhibited a variety of interests which he explored with concentrated effort. E used imaginative play activities with the greatest frequency, displaying more initiative in the development of his interests than any other child in the group. He *co-operated* in many of the contacts he made with other children, and accepted their leadership as frequently as he served as leader of the group. E developed his ideas in combination with K more frequently than with any other child in the group. He often asked J to join them in the development of an interest, but seldom paid any attention to younger members of the group. E engaged in *conflicts* with I and appeared to be greatly surprised when he discovered that I feared him. After his discovery, he used the original method or a similar one to scare I. Apparently, E never used this method of causing I to fear him in order to add to his prestige as a leader, but watched with interest I's reactions to certain suggestions and the confusion I exhibited in his contacts with other children.

J was eager to secure the attention of both adults and children in the Nursery School situations. She frequently resorted to teasing the younger children and demanding attention from adults by interrupting the adults in their activities or by offering excuses and lengthy explanations to adults who attempted to redirect her activities.

J's record shows that she exhibited each of the six behavior traits with approximately the same frequency as did E and K. These three children were in the group exhibiting *co-operation, initiation of activities,* and *resourcefulness* most frequently, and in the group demonstrating least frequently the traits, *resistance* and *aggressiveness*. J, E, and K showed *combative* behavior with approximately the same frequency, and were ranked among those children showing this behavior trait comparatively infrequently. J's contacts showed that she demonstrated *aggressiveness, co-operation,* and *combativeness* more frequently than did K and E. And E's records show that he *initiated activities* and *showed resourcefulness* in his contacts more frequently than any other of the fourteen children. E ranked last in the group when compared with the other members on the frequency with which he displayed *resistance* and *aggressiveness*.

E was considered an interesting child by all of the mothers. He was self-reliant and independent in routine and non-routine activities, asking for assistance infrequently. The practices used by the mothers in guiding E show fewer classified as *directs*, as was pointed out from K's record and is also true of the practices used in directing J. E was *warned* less frequently than any other member of the group, including J and K, and was *commended* and *reassured* more frequently than either of the other two children. There was no record of the use of the practice, *discourages*, in directing E. Practically the same distribution of the mothers' practices, *seeks information, offers explanation, diverts attention, urges,* and *forces*, prevailed in the case of E, and with about the same frequency as that recorded for the mothers in guiding J and K.

J was disliked by the majority of the mothers who served as assistants. She was considered a troublemaker in the group, a fact which may be partially explained by two conditions: First, J was the oldest member of the group and some of her *aggressive* activities may be attributed to her lack of interest in many of the activities of the other children; and, second, another contributing factor to J's eagerness for attention may have been the mother's keen interest in the older daughter, of whom she was extremely proud. This partiality left J the favorite of neither father nor mother, and caused her to be constantly striving for recognition and approval wherever they might be found from either adults or children with whom she came in contact.

MOTHER IX AND CHILDREN I AND H

This family consisted of the two boys, I and H, an older daughter, and the father and mother. The mother had no active interest beyond her family. The father was secure in business, having withstood the depression without serious financial difficulties. He maintained a temporary home in the city and a permanent home in the country. The family moved from the city to the country frequently, often, for convenience, choosing to rent a furnished apartment in the city and move there with only their personal belongings. Two maids were employed, one for the housekeeping and the other to take entire responsibility for the two boys, I and H.

Mother IX was very short and thin and seemed to possess much nervous energy. She always appeared tense in the contacts she made both with the children and with the mothers of the group. She showed friendliness for one mother and antagonism for two members of the group, and was passively indifferent toward the others. She showed very little interest in the school as a project, often criticizing certain mothers and the practices used by them when they acted as assistants.

Although Mother IX made frequent contacts with certain children in the group, the children's records as a whole show relatively infrequent verbal contacts with Mother IX.

The records of Mother IX show a prejudice in favor of her own children, H and I, in the frequency with which she used certain practices. *Urges* was never used when she directed I, seldom with H, and frequently with the remaining children of the group. She *encouraged* I relatively more often than she did H, and used this practice almost twice as frequently with her own children as with other members of the group. She *commended* I almost to the exclusion of other children within the group. Her practices of *discouragement* were directed to one child, K, the same child whom she omitted from the group when she selected to *commend, encourage, explain,* or *question.* However, K was included in the group which she guided by the use of the practice, *directs.*

The children who received the greatest proportion of this mother's practices were her own children and C, the child of a personal friend. She showed a decided dislike for K, E, and J, *overlooking* the advances they made to her and frequently using methods to *impede* the progress of their activities.

Mother IX, who apparently disliked routine duties, assumed the responsibilities of assistant in the Nursery School reluctantly. She showed her greatest interest in making the *rest* period successful, asking for more assistance from the experimenter than at any other time. The variety of methods used by her during this period would seem to indicate that she concentrated on making this situation a success.

Mother IX entered into the *free-play* situations, often suggesting activities which might interest certain children in the group and actively assisting I in making acceptable social contacts with other children.

The children seldom *failed in carrying out Mother IX's instructions.* Seemingly, they had no desire to question Mother IX's decisions and she offered no unnecessary explanations. She was unconcerned with regard to the interests expressed by the children and failed to recognize any *expression of disapproval*, except from I. The children *solved their problems independently* more frequently than they *solved them with assistance*, and *made requests for assistance* relatively infrequently.

H, who was the younger of the two children of Mother IX, was interested in very few activities. He showed no interest in any child in the group and seemed to be happiest when he was allowed to play with toys, usually trucks, engines, or trains, without the assistance of an adult. He *cried* most frequently in the *rest* situation, often to himself, although showing no *resistance* toward entering the situation. He approached the experimenter frequently and usually brought his toys to her vicinity. He *co-operated* with I more frequently than with any other child, and suggested the activity in which they *co-operated* more frequently than did I.

The behavior of H, who showed no dependence upon his mother and made no demands upon her attention, was in direct contrast to that of I, who frequently appealed to her for aid and protection. These appeals, as a rule, were confined to situations in which I tried to make social contacts with children older than himself. There were indications that I's behavior in such cases was due to his mother's attitude, for she was alert to all such situations, fearing for him and frequently coming to his aid.

I entered into *co-operative* contacts with E and K and sometimes with J, seeming to enjoy the play activities of this group more than those of any other. He was unable to follow the play activities of a group through to the end, usually withdrawing before the interest of the other children participating had been exhausted. He displayed a decided intolerance for younger members of the group, with the exception of H, his brother. He showed an intolerant attitude toward C, with whom he had frequent contacts outside of the school group. I showed much insecurity in the group, often accusing individuals of taking his toys, frequently shifting from one activity to another, and attempting to secure the attention of older members of the group. His mother, Mother IX, demonstrated a decided preference for I in interest and affection. She was very sensitive to the fact that she was small and expressed the fear that I, who resembled her, would also be small.

Both of her children seemed affected by the frequent moving of their possessions. They often asked their parents when they would move again and whether they would be allowed to take along certain prized possessions. I apparently was influenced in his behavior with other children by the fact that he was small, and always safeguarded himself and his possessions with care, frequently calling upon adults to protect him from any advances on the part of other children. He made frequent appeals to his mother when she served as assistant in the Nursery School, frequently guiding her attention to his attempts in securing notice from a group of children or from individuals in the group with whom he chose to *co-operate* in a play activity.

Apparently, the mothers serving as assistants in the group guided I's and H's activities when they observed a need. They exhibited no interest in their behavior or in any changes made by the children in their habits and interests. They frequently commented upon the interest that Mother IX showed in contacts with I and the apparent lack of interest in H. The majority of the mothers showed more interest in H than in I, which may be explained by the fact that H was the younger and by the seeming partiality that Mother IX showed toward I.

MOTHER X AND CHILD P

P was the only child in the family at the time this study was made. Mother X was trained for a profession which demanded adherence to rules and regulations without any consideration for personal preferences. P's father, in addition to his duties as a professional man, was an administrator of an institution. The family employed a full-time maid to care for the house. Aside from occasional social contacts, P's mother spent very little time outside the home, and had no special interests which she followed either inside or outside her home.

Mother X had had no experience with children before P was born. She was exacting with the child, demanding certain responses from her, and having little patience if she showed any tendency to diverge from the path which had been dictated by the mother.

The mother seemed to be an extrovert in all her reactions and frequently exhibited very strong emotion in response to P's behavior by speaking disparagingly of her conduct and activities. For instance, when P showed a tendency toward *dependence,* a characteristic which irritated the mother, her irritation was often expressed in harsh words, or by pushing the child into an activity which the mother considered interesting, or by the mother's withdrawal from the scene.

Mother X directed the children through routines with concise statements, often expressed as commands, to which she expected immediate, obedient response. She reminded the children of their responsibility in telling her of their physical needs, often interrupting an activity in which a child or a group of children were engaged to inquire as to those necessities. Mother X entered into the *free-play* situations more frequently than any other mother in the group, often directing the children in employing methods which she considered more effective in obtaining results than those in use. She directed P in the technique of making acceptable social contacts, frequently telling her that the method she had used was not the best, and suggesting a more effective one. She also directed P in taking care of her property and in looking after her personal rights, suggesting that the child had to protect herself.[5]

Mother X entered into any situation where *conflicts* arose or where any possibility of an· *emergency* existed, and *offered explanations, gave instructions,* and *encouraged* the children to follow her directions in the settlement of personal or group differences and in the avoidance of unpleasant results. Mother X frequently chose methods which prevented the child from making further progress in the activity.

The children seldom *failed in carrying out Mother X's instructions.* When confronted with *expressions of disapproval* from them, Mother X manifested interest in giving adequate explanations to support her suggestions. The children, seeming to sense a desire on the part of Mother X to help them, approached her with ease and *asked for information.* She expressed a willingness to *co-operate* with the children in many of the routine tasks which they undertook to solve. Her record shows a frequent occurrence of *crying,* and, upon investigation, these instances were found to be P's.

P was a stocky, very sturdy child who showed much interest in motor activities, accompanied by a lack of motor co-ordination. She was absorbed in pursuing a few interests and was greatly distracted from them by the presence of other children. She made many attempts at *co-operative play* with younger members of the group and showed satisfaction in the mutual development of interests. She frequently showed lack of skill in making contacts with members of the group, often making approaches that were

---

[5] There is some evidence that Mother X's emphasis upon developing social techniques and her concentrated effort to teach P to protect herself and her property rights were based upon the fact that P was an only child. The data of this study are inadequate, however, to prove this point conclusively.

too *aggressive* in nature, but was never antagonistic if the child repulsed her or withdrew.[6]

The mothers seemed not to be interested in P, and guided her through her routine activities and through the development of her play interests by practices classified as *directs*. P was not *questioned* by the mothers serving as assistants, and a few attempts were made to *divert her attention* by the use of those practices which would transfer her attention to a new activity. She was *commended* by the mothers and *reassured* frequently in her contacts with the adults. The mothers as a group did not choose the practices used by P's mother in guiding P, omitting those classified as *urges, forces, impedes, warns,* and *discourages,* all of which were chosen by Mother X.

MOTHER XI AND CHILD Q

This family, Mother XI, Q, and the father, was forced, because of the effects of the depression upon the father's profession, to live with relatives. The child was constantly reminded of the noise she made and was not allowed, because of the lack of room, to play freely with her toys. Q shared a small bedroom with her parents, and this bedroom represented the only place where she had any freedom.

The father was in a disturbed state of mind over the financial condition of the family at the time this study was made. The mother was constantly reminded by her friends and relatives that on this account she must not show any signs of worry. She was intensely devoted to Q and in sympathy with the child's problems, frequently explaining that Q had not had a chance to develop normally.

Mother XI was quiet and always agreeable to the children and adults with whom she made contacts. She appeared to be de-

[6] P was given the prescribed two weeks for orientation to the Nursery School, but she entered the school after it had been in session three months. The behavior of P, which showed in many instances a lack of orientation to the Nursery School and to the children in the group, was much more noticeable against the background of the behavior of children who had been in the Nursery School for a longer period.

pressed at times, but never attempted to secure sympathy from anyone. Mother XI showed much interest in all of the children of the Nursery School. She asked for frequent conferences with the experimenter and discussed the children's problems from the point of view of remedial methods already in use or that could be used to advantage. She showed an interest, but not an exclusive one, in Q and her problems.

Mother XI's records of practices show much emphasis placed upon her explanations to the children and upon the information she secured from them. At the same time she *encouraged* the children, and made suggestions for more desirable activities than they were pursuing.

Mother XI showed much interest in making the *instructional* periods in the Nursery School interesting to the children. She was active in giving instructions throughout the *free-play* period, in demonstrating the use of toys and of play equipment, and in helping the children to develop acceptable social techniques. She spent much of her time in emphasizing the solution of these problems to Q.[7]

Mother XI's record shows that the children expressed *resistance* verbally more frequently with her than with any other mother. The children also *attacked others* more frequently, and *cried* more often with Mother XI than with any other mother. These forms of behavior observed in the children's activities seemed to be explained by the mother's lack of confidence in herself and in her practices; hence, the use of practices which seemed to indicate indecision. These qualities of Mother XI's guidance seemed to be disturbing to the children's interest in constructive activities.

Q was disturbed over any changes in the activities or in the routine situations and by the presence and absence of adults in the group. Q frequently expressed her needs, with the apparent purpose of keeping her mother occupied in supplying them. The

---

[7] As in P's case, Q entered the Nursery School late, six months after it had opened. Any behavior not acceptable to the children or the adults in the group was further emphasized by the different behavior of the other children in the group.

mother was requested by the experimenter to explain her duties to Q and thus to give the child the basis for the mother's attention to other children and for any absence from the group. These methods proved successful in helping Q to adjust herself to the Nursery School, and to the development of interest in the activities of other children, as well as concentrating upon her own interests. The experimenter proposed other methods of treating this behavior problem from the standpoint of a feeling of insecurity in the child. These data are inadequate as a basis for a conclusion that Q's behavior was the result of the insecurity of the family. However, a subsequent observation, when Q's family had made adjustments and found freedom and security in their home, showed an absence of many of these undesirable activities. This opinion was further substantiated by the fact that a pediatrician under whose care she had been placed, explained to the experimenter that Q's illness was due to the strained conditions in the home and not to any physical defect. As soon as Q had made adjustments to the Nursery School and was able to have freedom in her activities and in contacts with other children, her problem, which had been one of eating, disappeared and she was dismissed by the physician.

Q engaged in *combative* behavior more frequently than any other member of the group, and the records show that she initiated the conflicts more often than she participated in similar contacts initiated by other children. Those contacts classified as *aggressiveness* were also frequent in her behavior, and here, too, she was predominantly the initiator instead of the participant.

Q appealed to the mothers serving as assistants as an interesting, alert child capable of making improvements in her behavior, if given an opportunity. The mothers directed many of their practices classified as *commends* and *reassures* toward Q. There was no evidence of any disapproval or impatience shown by any of the mothers toward Q's behavior, and they spent time and energy explaining the Nursery School equipment and the activities of the adults and children to her. She was *encouraged* to explore interests she initiated and frequently the adults attempted to guide her by simple directions.

DISCUSSION OF ABOVE SUMMARIES

The foregoing accounts of the various mothers and their children are obviously sketchy, and reflect only the information available to the investigator. Since the available information was limited, and since the sketches show a great deal of individual variation, it is impossible to derive any definitive generalizations or conclusions from the material. In the writer's judgment, however, the sketches do reveal some general trends. It appears that the assisting mothers can roughly be divided into three groups, according to practices employed in directing the children.

The characteristics of one group of mothers were as follows: Their methods of guidance indicated an active interest in understanding children's behavior; they exhibited fewer prejudices toward individual children, and less frequently showed predilections toward experimental use of equipment and of certain social techniques than did other mothers who served as assistants; their attention was apparently focused on the difficulties the child or children were attempting to overcome or on the adjustment the individual or group was making. This group of mothers used guidance which was specific in that the methods were apparently chosen to assist the individual with his or her problems.

Another group of mothers seemed to restrict the activities of the children to those the adult judged interesting and profitable for the child to pursue. They insisted upon the child's using methods approved by the adult. The contacts of the mothers in this group revealed prejudices in favor of and against certain children; their practices showed that they were afraid of allowing the children freedom because of fear associated with the experimental use of equipment and because of their lack of understanding of the child's method of establishing group relationships with those about him. The members of this group directed the children more frequently than did the other mothers, demanding immediate and explicit compliance to their directions. In the guidance techniques that they employed, they seemed to overlook the individual's problems. The children depended upon these mothers to initiate their play activities, and the children demonstrated greater dependence in routine situations.

The contacts of the third group of mothers with the children in the Nursery School indicated that, apparently, they regarded the school as a place where their child and other children would develop skills in the use of equipment and learn satisfactory techniques in group relationships because of the proximity of equipment and through their contacts with children of their own age group. They seemed to regard adult guidance as unnecessary and unwise, and apparently believed that children should be left free to work out the solution to their own difficulties. It was apparent that this theory had limitations in that the mothers failed to recognize that the child may be *guided* into making satisfactory adjustments and developing acceptable techniques and behavior traits.

Furthermore, a study of the mothers' practices tended to reveal a pattern for directing children that showed differences in the choice and in the frequency with which individual children were guided by the practices. Likewise, the children's activities tended toward patterns of behavior which seemed to show the children's response to adult instructions. A comparison of the six factors of behavior exhibited by each child in contacts with other children tended to reveal a pattern of behavior which was peculiar to the individual.

Chapter VIII
GENERAL SUMMARY

THIS investigation dealt with the practices of mothers and the activities of children in a co-operative nursery school. The specific purpose was to study (1) the practices used by the mothers in the situations observed, (2) the activities of a child or of children in situations in which the mothers participated, (3) the behavior of a child or of children as shown in their contacts with other children, and (4) the language used by mothers in guiding the children in the situations under observation.

Eleven mothers and fourteen children were participants in the Co-operative Nursery School organized by the mothers. The school was located in the home of one of the parents where provisions were made for routine activities and for the development of a variety of play interests. The mothers, with the exception of one, accepted assignments in the Nursery School, each serving as assistant to the experimenter.

Three three-hour observation records were made of the eleven mothers and of the fourteen children as they participated in the general routine and non-routine activities of the Nursery School. A record was made of the activities of a particular mother or child assigned to the observer for observation, describing the overt behavior exhibited by each as expressed by movements, by the choice and use of equipment, and by any verbalization that took place. Records were also made of the activities of those children in the group who made contacts with the mother or with the child under observation during the particular period.

Each mother was observed during one three-hour period the first day she acted as assistant in the Nursery School and during two additional three-hour periods, with one day intervening, during the first week she was present at the school. The nine hours of observation allotted each child were scheduled as follows: one three-hour period before the child's own mother acted as assistant, one three-hour period at the time the child's own mother was acting as assistant, and a final three-hour period scheduled at the time another mother was assisting. No record was made of a child's activities until he had been in attendance at the Nursery School a minimum of two weeks.

Practices used by the mothers were classified according to thirteen categories. Practices that could be classified under the general heading, *directs,* occurred with the greatest frequency, both in composite records of the group and in each of the individual records of the eleven mothers. *Directs* constituted 51.8 per cent of the total number of practices and ranged in use from 57.8 per cent in Mother IV's record to 39.8 per cent in that of Mother V.

The remaining twelve practices could be grouped in six pairs, as follows, when arranged according to frequency in the records of the eleven mothers : *seeks information* and *offers explanation, impedes* and *encourages, overlooks* and *commends, diverts attention* and *urges, reassures* and *warns, discourages* and *forces.* Seven of the mothers employed all thirteen practices, and with about the same relative frequency, as shown by the tabulations from the composite records of the group. In four records there were no instances of practices classified as *forces* and *discourages.*

The practices, *seeks information, offers explanation, directs, encourages, impedes,* and *overlooks,* were utilized with all fourteen children and were used by all the mothers in the eight routine and non-routine situations. The records of the practices revealed the omission of the following practices in the various situations indicated : In *care of wraps and exchange of clothing,* the practices, *forces* and *discourages,* were not used; three practices, *diverts attention, reassures,* and *discourages,* were not observed during the *mid-morning lunch* periods; during the *rest* periods there were no practices classed as *warns;* in situations in which *conflicts* occurred, the mothers omitted *warns, discourages,* and *reassures.*

The practice, *directs,* was most frequently used with all the children. The four practices, *encourages, impedes, seeks information,* and *offers explanation,* were each observed with comparable frequency in each of the children's records. Practices classified as *forces, reassures,* and *discourages* were shown relatively infrequently in all the children's records.

At one extreme was a child who, during the period covered by the data which were analyzed quantitatively, received attention 546 times, and at the other, a child who received attention 172 times as indicated by records of mothers' practices. Some practices were used relatively more often than others in the assistance of different children. The details concerning practices used with individual children were presented in Table III.

The "average" mother made relatively more use of the practices, *overlooks, seeks information, offers explanation, encourages, commends,* and *warns,* when directing her own child. When directing the children of other mothers the "average" mother made relatively more use of the practices, *reassures, diverts attention, impedes, directs, urges, forces,* and *discourages.*

The records of the children's activities revealed that they were *able successfully to carry out the mothers' instructions* with a high degree of frequency. The children's activities exhibited *failure in carrying out mothers' instructions* relatively infrequently, when compared with the number of times they *succeeded in carrying out the mothers' instructions.* The children's activity records revealed *success* in each of the situations, while *failure to carry out instructions* was not observed in the *mid-morning lunch* situations and in situations in which *conflicts* occurred.

The presence of children other than her own induced a greater variety of practices from the mother than did the presence of her own child.

Certain aspects of the behavior of children in their contacts with one another were classified under six headings; these classes in the order of frequency of occurrence were as follows: (1) *resistance,* (2) *co-operation,* (3) *aggressiveness,* (4) *initiation of activity,* (5) *resourcefulness,* and (6) *combativeness.* As would be expected, there were individual differences between the children in the relative frequency of these forms of behavior.

Resourcefulness was displayed more often when the child's own mother was present than at the time other mothers assisted in the school. Children's contacts with one another exhibited *co-operation, resistance, aggressiveness, initiation of activities,* and *combativeness* more often in the presence of other mothers than when their own mothers were assisting.

A comparison of mothers' ratings of the children's tendency to display each of the six forms of behavior with the frequency with which the children exhibited each behavior during the observation periods indicated many discrepancies between the ratings and the objective data. These discrepancies between ratings assigned to the children by their own mothers and ratings assigned by other mothers are shown in some detail in graphs in the main body of the study.

As compared with objective records, the mothers tended to overrate the frequency with which their own children exhibited *aggressiveness* and *initiation of activity* and to underrate the behavior factors classified as *co-operation, resistance, combativeness,* and *resourcefulness* in the conduct of their own children. When rating children other than their own, the mothers tended to overrate five of the behavior traits, *co-operation, resistance, aggressiveness, combativeness,* and *initiation of activity,* and to underrate the frequency with which the children showed *resourcefulness* in their contacts with other children.

A study of the number of words used by the mothers in directing the children revealed differences ranging from 3,283 words at the time Mother VI was observed to 1,750 words in Mother II's record. Equally wide variation was observed in the number of words spoken by the children at the time the different mothers were assistants. The greatest number of words, 663, were recorded for the children when Mother XI was assistant, and the smallest number, 189, were shown when Mother IV was present. Some variation in the amount of talking by the children would be expected by virtue of the fact that there is usually an increase with age in the use of language apart from the factor of changes in adult supervision.

The mothers differed considerably in relative frequency of their use of declarative, interrogative, and imperative sentence forms and in the frequency with which they expressed their practices in positive and negative statements.

The records do not reveal any consistent relationship between the amount of talking by the child and the number of words shown in the mothers' records, the type of sentences chosen by them, and their use of negative and positive suggestions.

Summary accounts of the outstanding general characteristics of the individual mothers, of the practices they used in directing the children, and of characteristics exhibited by the mothers' own children are presented in the immediately preceding chapter of this study.

BIBLIOGRAPHY

1. Ackerley, Lois. *Information and Attitudes Regarding Child Development Possessed by Parents of Elementary School Children.* Vol. III, Research in Parent Education, University of Iowa, Iowa City, Iowa, 1934.

2. Chassell, J. O. *Experience Variable.* A Study of Variable Factors in Experience Contributing to the Formation of Personality. J. O. Chassell, Publisher, Rochester, New York, 1928.

3. Dennis, Lemo T. *A Descriptive Study of Family Relationships from the Viewpoint of Child Guidance and Parent Education.* Ph.D. Dissertation, Cornell University, Ithaca, New York, 1931.

4. Humphrey, Laura J. *A Study of the Relationship of Selected Factors in the Home Environment to Play Behavior.* Research in Parent Education, University of Iowa, Iowa City, Iowa, 1938.

5. Jack, Lois. *A Device for Measurement of Parents' Attitudes and Practices.* Research in Parent Education, Vol. I. University of Iowa, Iowa City, Iowa, 1934.

6. Lashley, Karl S. *et al. Studies on Dynamics of Behavior.* Reaction Tendencies Relating to Personality and Measuring Traits in Delinquency. University of Chicago Press, Chicago, 1932.

7. Laws, Gertrude. *Parent-Child Relationships.* Contributions to Education, No. 283. Bureau of Publications, Teachers College, Columbia University, New York City, 1927.

8. Maller, J. B. *Character and Personality Tests.* Teachers College, Columbia University, New York City, 1932.

9. Ojeman, Ralph H. *Measurement of Attitude Toward Self-Reliance.* Research in Parent Education, Vol. III. Iowa University, Iowa City, Iowa, 1934.

10. Schaus, Hazel. *A Device for Measurement of Parents' Attitudes and Practices.* Research in Parent Education, Vol. I. University of Iowa, Iowa City, Iowa, 1934.

11. Stogdill, Ralph M. "Parental Attitudes and Mental Hygiene Standards," *Mental Hygiene,* Vol. XV, pp. 813-827, 1931.

12. Tilson, Agnes. *The Problems of the Pre-School Child.* Contributions to Education, No. 356. Bureau of Publications, Teachers College, Columbia University, New York City, 1929.

13. Watson, Goodwin. "Happiness Among Adult Students of Education." *Journal of Educational Psychology,* Vol. XXI, pp. 79-109, February, 1930.

14. Wickman, E. K. *Children's Behavior and Teachers' Attitudes.* The Commonwealth Fund, New York City, 1928.

Date Due

Due	Returned	Due	Returned
NOV 30 1987			